Contents

What Great Chefs Know That You Don't

Harlequin Books

TORONTO • NEW YORK • LONDON
AMSTERDAM • PARIS • SYDNEY • HAMBURG
STOCKHOLM • ATHENS • TOKYO • MILAN
MADRID • WARSAW • BUDAPEST • AUCKLAND

ISBN 0-373-80513-6

WHAT GREAT CHEFS KNOW THAT YOU DON'T

Designed by Tim Cooper of **Proteus Design.**

This edition published by arrangement with Harlequin Books S.A.

Introduction

Everyone appreciates a great meal, and many of us would love to be able to prepare one. We buy cookbooks by the carload, watch television cooking shows and trade recipes as if they were stock certificates. And yet, somehow, the ability to prepare great meals consistently eludes us. What's missing? In a word, the missing ingredient is understanding.

You see, nothing is so misunderstood as the art of cooking. As the great chefs will attest, fine cooking is at once far more complex and far simpler than most people realize. It is more complex because of the understanding required to bring a truly great meal to the table—an understanding of tools, materials and the culture from which the cuisine originated. And it is simpler because once you understand the basics, many fabulous meals can be prepared in a matter of minutes.

So, how to get this "understanding"? With our busy lives and family commitments, most of us don't have the time to apprentice ourselves to a fabulous chef in a four-star restaurant. That's why **Harlequin Ultimate Guides** has prepared *What Great Chefs Know That You Don't*.

It's not a cookbook in the usual sense; there are very few recipes sprinkled throughout its pages. It is a book that introduces you to the fundamentals of fine cooking as seen through the eyes of master chefs. Among other things, you will learn how to shop like a professional: identifying and selecting great ingredients is the first step toward a fabulous culinary experience. And you will learn how to increase your chances of success in the kitchen by selecting proper equipment. There's much more, of course: chapters on kitchen shortcuts, healthy substitutions, fabulous presentation and tips on avoiding culinary disasters.

Will reading *What Great Chefs Know That You Don't* make you a gourmet chef? Probably not, unless you become so inspired that you do finally secure a coveted apprenticeship. What it will do, however, is give you the background to step into your kitchen with confidence, knowing you're truly prepared.

CHAPTER ONE

Supermarkets
&
Super Menus

The Early Bird Catches the Tenderloin

Setting Up a Great Kitchen

Most great meals begin in the market in the early hours before dawn. Every great city has large outdoor markets carrying fish, meat, fruit and vegetables fresh from farms and fishing boats. There, amidst the exhilarating sights and smells of the market, you will find chefs and their provisioners, searching for the freshest fish, the best cuts of meat and the finest vegetables available.

Why are they up so early after working late the previous evening? Because one of

COOKING TIP #1 FROM THE CHEFS

WHERE'S THE (GOOD) BEEF?

Forced to buy supermarket meat? Here are a few tips to help you find the best available:

- Good cuts of beef should look silky, not wet.
- Rolled cuts should be tied, not skewered, to preserve moisture.
- Barding, the thin layer of fat found on the outside of a roast, should cover the roast completely.
- Bones be sawed through cleanly, leaving no jagged edges.
- All excess fat should be removed.
- Ground beef should be red. A pink color indicates a high percentage of fat.

the keys to gourmet cooking is great ingredients. Great chefs know that if you shop with care and discernment, your work is half done. As consummate professionals, chefs also have a great appreciation for the tools of their trade—the same way painters love their brushes and canvases, and sculptors their stones and chisels.

Marketing for the Rest of Us

Admittedly, shuffling around New York's Fulton Fish Market at 5:00 AM looking for Atlantic salmon is something most of us would live without, even if it was practical. But there's no reason why we can't apply the wisdom and practiced eye of the professional chef when we go to the neighborhood supermarket or fish store.

First of all, let's talk about stores. Why do you shop at the local MegaFood Mart? Is it because of their "everyday low prices," coupons, a great produce section, or just simple convenience? Unfortunately, the vast majority of supermarkets are much better at pushing soaps and prepackaged fast foods than they are at supplying quality ingredients. If you're really interested in improving your cooking, you'll do well to look beyond these air-conditioned emporiums with their wide linoleum aisles.

In almost every community there are alternatives: farmers' markets full of fresh produce, old-fashioned butcher shops, gourmet supermarkets, natural food stores, and quality fish stores. And of course, during the summer months, there's the backyard garden for succulent table vegetables. But even if you're one of those rare individuals without access to alternatives, don't despair. We'll show you how to identify the best foods available regardless of where you buy them.

Finding a Good Butcher

Professional chefs and gifted amateurs alike swear that finding a good butcher is just as important to their well-being as finding a good family physician. And these days, they seem much harder to find.

So, how can you tell if you've found a

COOKING TIP #2
FROM THE CHEFS

WHY AGED MEAT
IS WORTH THE EXPENSE

Meat is aged by hanging carcasses in refrigeration chambers. Beef is usually aged 10 to 14 days and lamb roughly 4 days, during which time moisture evaporates from the meat, reducing its weight. More importantly, however, aging allows enzymes in the meat to break down the tough connective tissues, greatly improving both the taste and tenderness of the meat.

good butcher? First of all, he's probably doing an excellent business. Great professionals in any field are usually discovered by the public sooner or later. Second, good butchers usually buy meat by the carcass and hang it until properly aged. If you're not sure whether your butcher ages his own beef, ask him. Third, good butchers

COOKING TIP #3 FROM THE CHEFS

QUICK TIPS ON POULTRY AND OTHER MEATS

- Poultry — Unfortunately, good poultry is terribly hard to find. The best birds are free-range chicken and turkey, which are allowed to wander around the barnyard. Because of the variety in their diets and the ability to move around, these birds have less fat and a much more pronounced flavor than their barn-raised cousins.

- Veal — Good milk-fed veal should be firm and moist and very pale pink in color. Red meat indicates the calf had been allowed to grow too old. Avoid cuts with too much marbling: it indicates overfeeding.

- Pork — Choose cuts that have plenty of lean flesh and that are pearly white in color.

- Lamb — Look for very lean, rosy-colored meat with white fat. Avoid meat with crumbly or discolored fat.

offer their customers a wider variety of cuts than supermarkets. Fourth, good butchers can be more expensive than regular markets. It's worth the extra cost because they don't take shortcuts and only deal in quality products. If you haven't purchased cuts of meat from a good butcher, you will soon come to know and value the considerable difference in quality and taste.

Try a Little Tenderness

Everyone loves a tender piece of meat, but most people don't realize what makes it tender in the first place. As your butcher will tell you, selecting the right cuts of meat goes a long way toward getting a dish that melts in your mouth. The determining factor is exercise. The more exercise a muscle group receives, the more connective tissue it develops, and the tougher the meat is. Cuts from the hindquarters and loins are typically where the best and most tender meat is found.

As a rule of thumb, the more connective tissue a piece of meat has, the more cooking required to break down the connective tissue and render the meat tender. This is why tougher cuts such as rump, chuck and flank steaks are usually prepared by way of braising, stewing or boiling.

Other ways to make tough meat tender are to use marinades or to pound the meat with a mallet. Both techniques work to break up connective tissue. Marinades break down the tissue through the acids contained in lemon juice, vinegar or wine. Mallets break down the tissue through the simple act of pounding.

Netting the Bounty of the Sea

Now that you've made a lifelong friend of your butcher, it's time to locate a good fish store. Don't tell your butcher, but if anything, a good fish store is more indispensable than the butcher shop. It's increasingly difficult to find decent selections of fish in supermarkets these days. If you've never eaten amberjack, pompano or black sea bass, you simply have no idea of how extraordinary fish can taste. But it must be fresh!

Here's how you tell fresh from stale. Basically, fresh fish look like they just jumped out of the water into your boat. Their eyes are bright and have solid black pupils, and their gills are clean and bright red. Stale fish typically have dull, discolored eyes and have no sheen to their skin. Their gills are dark and slimy and they often smell fishy as well. To ensure freshness, most experts recommend selecting fish before it is filleted. If that is not possible, you must find a reliable fish dealer with a brisk business. Frankly, the more traffic a fish dealer has, the less likely there will be any stale fish on the premises.

Tracking the Wild Truffle

The first step in purchasing quality fruits and vegetables is to find a place that sells them. Once again, that is probably not your local supermarket. Fortunately,

COOKING TIP #4 FROM THE CHEFS

FOOLPROOF CANTALOUPE

There's more confusion about selecting good cantaloupes or muskmelons than any other fruit. Buy in season, between the months of May and September, and look for:

- Thick, coarse veining that readily stands out
- Yellowish-buff skin between the veining
- Pleasing aroma of cantaloupe
- A symmetrical shallow depression where the stem was
- Slightly soft skin on the ends of the cantaloupe

most areas of the country have thriving farmers' markets these days. Many areas also have natural food supermarkets, so there's no reason to settle for bland vegetables. If you've never shopped at a farmers' market, make an excursion out of it. Take along your family or a friend and explore the wonderful world of truly fresh food.

Generally, the experts will tell you that if a food looks good, the chances are it will taste good as well. This guideline works pretty well with fruits and vegetables, but there are some exceptions. When buying vegetables:

★ Look for crispness and bright colors
★ Buy vegetables at the height of their season to ensure quality, taste and value
★ To avoid waste, buy no more than you will use in three to four days
★ Avoid vegetables with any visible signs of decay

Quality asparagus, for example, has a fresh appearance with closed, compact tips and rich green spears. If the tips are open and spread out or decayed in any way, pass them by. They will undoubtedly be tough and lacking in flavor.

Fruit Guidelines

Buying fruit is not significantly different from buying vegetables. In both cases, you should select produce that is rich in color and looks fresh. You also need to be vigilant about any signs of decay, and buy only what you can use without waste. Experts suggest buying fruit in season to secure the best-tasting product at the lowest price.

However, even if you follow all these guidelines, there are fewer guarantees with fruit than with vegetables. Sometimes fruit that looks great tastes mealy, bitter or bland because it's overly mature or has been subjected briefly to freezing temperatures. Occasionally, you will also find cosmetically challenged fruit that is a delight to the palate. This is especially true if you shop at farmers' markets and natural food stores where good fruit doesn't have to be the most perfect-looking fruit on the shelf.

Organic Produce

Like fine wine, produce resonates with the flavors native to the soil in which it is grown. If it is grown in soil nurtured by composting, mulching and other natural fertilizers, as well as time-honored techniques such as crop rotation, the produce will have a deep, rich taste. On the other hand, if the vegetable or fruit is the product of farming that depends heavily on chemical fertilizers and genetically altered seeds, it may be as appetizing as cardboard shirt backings.

As we've already mentioned, farmers' markets are sometimes a good solution to this quandary, but even then you don't know if the farmers are raising crops chemically or traditionally. The best bet for pure, rich-tasting vegetables and fruit is one of the natural food supermarkets springing up around the country. More and more of them have comprehensive organic produce sections worth frequenting. It's also worth noting that organic farmers raise more varieties of familiar

COOKING TIP #5 FROM THE CHEFS

A PLACE FOR EVERYTHING, AND EVERYTHING IN ITS PLACE

Professional bartenders are marvels of precision, making hundreds of drinks an hour on busy nights while hardly looking at the bottles. What's their secret? **The Speed Rack** – a metal rack below the surface of the bar that allows them to place their hands on the right bottle of liquor without having to move a step. Try to organize your kitchen the same way, so you can find anything you need without having to look or move around too much. And once you've organized, make sure you keep everything in the same place.

produce than chemical farmers, so you could be in for some pleasant surprises.

A word of caution, however. Since organic

produce is raised without the benefit of chemical pesticides and fertilizers, it's more expensive and isn't always as pretty as the competition. The taste is usually well worth the small sacrifice in cost and looks.

Spices of Life

Next to great produce and fine cuts of meat, the most important ingredients any discerning chef can have are fresh herbs and spices. You can find top-quality spices the same way you find quality produce, by looking for fresh products bursting with aroma and color. Keep your herbs and spices in a cool, dark place such as a pantry to preserve their flavor and color. Buy in small quantities and replace as you use them.

Here are the basic herbs and spices experts consider essential for fine cooking.

ALLSPICE
Berry of a Caribbean tree that combines the flavors of cinnamon, clove and nutmeg.

Used primarily for cakes, cookies, pies, puddings and breads.

BASIL, FRESH OR DRIED
Bitter, clove-flavored relative of mint.
Complements any tomato dish.
Used widely in Italian and French cooking.

BAY LEAVES
Woody flavored with faint hint of cinnamon.
Used with meat, fish and poultry.

CARAWAY SEEDS
Nutty with slight licorice flavor.
Used in breads, cheeses, vegetables such as cabbage and sauerkraut.

CAYENNE PEPPER
Ground hot red pepper of the Capsicum family.
Adds heats and flavor to Latin American and Southwestern cuisines.

CHILI POWDER
Pungent ground mixture of chili pep-

pers and other spices such as oregano, cumin, garlic and clove. Varies from mild to very hot.
Used in Latin American, Asian and Southwestern cuisines.

CINNAMON, GROUND AND STICK
Sweet and slightly hot bark of the cassia tree.
Used mainly for baking, spicy sauces and to add spicy flavor to drinks.

CLOVES, WHOLE AND GROUND
Flower buds of the clove tree.
Used in cakes, pies, puddings, spicy sauces and drinks.

CORIANDER, FRESH, SEEDS OR GROUND
Nut-like seed of a plant in the parsley family.
Used extensively in Latin American and Southwestern cuisines.

CUMIN, SEEDS OR GROUND
Strongly flavored and similar to caraway.
Used in chili and curry powders and is a

principal ingredient of Latin American and Southwestern cuisines.

CURRY POWDER
A mixture of anywhere from 16 to 20 spices including cinnamon, clove, cumin, ginger, black and red pepper, turmeric and fenugreek.
Used as a basic spice for Indian cooking and for salad and egg dishes.

DILL
Tart herb with a taste of lemon.
Used with fish, eggs, cheeses, salads, cucumbers and tomatoes.

MARJORAM
A milder relative of the oregano family with a mellow-nutty bouquet.
Used with veal, lamb, poultry, tomatoes and potatoes.

MUSTARD POWDER
Hot and spicy ground mustard seed.
Used in sauces, pickles, salad dressings and deviled foods.

NUTMEG
Mellow, sweet and nutty in flavor.
Used as an all-purpose spice with many applications.

OREGANO
Wild version of marjoram with a bitter flavor.
Used extensively in Italian cooking for sauces.

PAPRIKA
A milder pepper of the Capsicum family, reddish in color and slightly sweet.
Used in Hungarian cooking.

PARSLEY
Fresh tasting and full of flavor.
Used as an all-purpose seasoning in many cuisines.

BLACK PEPPERCORNS AND GROUND BLACK PEPPER
The dried, unhusked, immature berries from the pepper vine.
Most pungent and biting of the peppercorn family.

Used so extensively it's called the "master spice."

WHITE PEPPERCORNS AND GROUND WHITE PEPPER

The dried inner core of ripe pepper berries, less pungent and spicy.
Used for lighter pepper flavoring in soups and sauces.

HOT RED-PEPPER FLAKES

Flaked version of the pepper plant. Very spicy.
Used to provide pockets of heat in sauces and to enliven salads, pizza, and meat dishes.

ROSEMARY

Very lemony with a slight flavor of resin.
Used in meat dishes, salads and with vegetables, especially potatoes.

SAFFRON

Dried orange stigma of the saffron crocus. Exotic and medicinal in flavor and very expensive.

Used extensively in Spanish cuisines. Adds flavor and color.

TARRAGON
Strong licorice flavor.
Used extensively for seafood, salad, eggs and dressings.

THYME
Minty and tea-like in flavor.
Another all-purpose spice used extensively in many cuisines.

VANILLA EXTRACT
Sweet and perfume-like flavor. From the seed of a Mexican orchid.
Used primarily in baking.

The Kitchen as an Art Studio

Good Equipment Is Worth What It Costs

Most of the large packaged-food companies have extensive "test kitchens," places where they try out new recipes containing their products. To professional chefs, these places are more like factories or laboratories than kitchens.

For the chef, the kitchen is not just a workshop, but an atelier, a studio where great works of art are conceived and created. What's the difference between a studio and a workshop? Attitude and purpose.

Like painters, sculptors and other artists, great chefs believe that their working areas must be orchestrated so that nothing interferes with the act of creation. Their kitchens are laid out so that there are no extra steps and so that the chefs can lay their hands on virtually anything they need with their eyes closed. And when they pick up a tool, whether it's a wire whisk or a paring knife, they have absolute confidence that the tool is the best available for the job.

Obviously, not everyone can afford to spend a fortune re-creating the kitchen of a four-star restaurant in their homes. You should endeavor, however, to outfit your kitchen with the finest implements you can afford. In the end, good equipment offers the best value because it performs better and it lasts indefinitely, if properly cared for.

Now We're Cooking with Gas

Comparing a professional chef's range to the average domestic stove is like comparing a go-cart to a grand prix car. Yes, a professional range is more expensive. But if you're serious about cooking and have the space and finances, you should have a professional range as the centerpiece of your kitchen. It offers more burners, ovens and storage space, more control over temperature—and it lasts longer. Some ranges are now available especially converted for home use.

Obviously, buying a professional range is not an option for everyone. But in most areas of the country you're offered a choice between gas and electric ranges. Experts universally prefer gas ranges because a flick of the knob provides instant heat control over a wide range of temperatures. So, if you're using electric now, consider switching to gas when it's time to replace your range.

Cutlery and Other Sharp Stuff

Many chefs believe that good knives are the single most important tools they own. Knives allow them to create dishes requiring precision carving and save untold amounts of time in preparation. Yet, if you explore the average domestic kitchen, you will be hard-pressed to find a single decent knife.

You can't have too many good knives, but you only need two quality blades to get started—a small paring knife and a large knife for carving meat and chopping vegetables.

Knives are made one of two ways. They are stamped out of a sheet of steel using a pattern (die-cut), or they are forged. Forged blades are made from a single piece of steel that is first heated to a high temperature, then hammered into the shape of a knife. The steel is then hardened by alternate applications of heat and cold. The forged knife tends to have a front-weighted blade that makes it easier to cut through difficult substances such as gristle and bone.

Stamped blades, on the other hand, tend to be back-weighted and lighter in the hand. The user has to work harder to accomplish the same thing. Although they are more expensive, master chefs will use nothing but forged blades.

Ideally, your knives should not only be forged but should be constructed of high-carbon stainless steel, a material renowned for holding a good edge as well as resisting discoloration and rust. Another reason to consider stainless steel blades is that vegetables such as onions and shallots are very "acid" and discolor readily if chopped with blades constructed of non-stainless steel.

Cutting Boards

No well-equipped kitchen is complete without a decent cutting board. Although traditionalists prefer laminated maple or butcher-block boards, increasingly the experts are switching to polyethylene boards as their material of choice. They are easier to clean and can even be placed in the dishwasher, and they are not plagued by the bacteria buildup common to wooden cutting surfaces. Good polyethylene boards also make terrific surfaces for rolling out dough for pie crusts and other confections.

Although polyethylene boards are usually 1/4 inch or 1/2 inch thick, you can find 3/4-

COOKING TIP #6 FROM THE CHEFS

THE CUTTING EDGE

To keep your cutting board from shifting while you are working on it, place a damp cloth or thin piece of foam rubber under the board.

If you can't give up that maple cutting board, sanitize it with periodic trips to the microwave. Zap it for 60 seconds on high and your old board will be bacteria free.

inch-thick boards at better shops. The thicker boards hold up much better in high dishwasher temperatures.

Saucepans, Skillets and Pots

As with knives, you don't need a huge collection of pots and pans to create great dishes, but it's absolutely essential that you purchase the best quality you can afford.

Like most things in life, you get what you pay for when it comes to kitchen equipment. It's far better to have a few really good pots than a large collection of mediocre ones.

Experts suggest that you can get by very well with only a few items. Buy a large and a small skillet; a large saucepan suitable for making pasta, soups, and stews; a medium-size saucepan; and a small saucepan.

It's relatively easy to tell a good pot from a bad one. First of all, good pots and pans are almost always thick, if not heavy. That's because most cooking requires temperature regulation and uniform distribution of heat—something impossible in thin-walled pots and pans. Food prepared in skillets constructed of thin metal runs an excellent chance of burning unless watched very closely.

If you have a very modest budget and don't mind putting a little more elbow grease into cleaning your utensils, it's hard to beat old-fashioned iron skillets and pots. They're heavy, cumbersome and will rust if you're not careful, but they do a great job of distributing heat.

The next step up in price and quality are the enamel-coated cast-iron skillets, followed by professional quality pots and pans made with walls of aluminum and stainless steel sandwiched together. Top of the line? The expensive heavy copper pots and pans lined with tin.

The Mysterious Art of Menu Planning

Pick a Style That Matches Your Temperament

There are as many approaches to menu planning as there are chefs. Some plan as carefully as if they were preparing for a moon flight. Others prefer serendipity, letting the menu present itself to them as they absorb the aromas and sights of the market. Listed below are a number of individual approaches that help provide structure for menu preparation. Of course, in the final analysis, only you can decide which style or combination is for you.

The Traditionalist – Even in this day and

age, when you can find fresh produce at any time of the year, some cooks work by the calendar. They prefer to cook heartier dishes, such as stews and roasts, in winter, and lighter dishes in summer. They use locally grown ingredients whenever possible.

The Economist – This chef bases menus on what's available in the markets at good prices. The approach takes a lot of planning, and calls for designing meals based on specials and seasonable vegetables. The economist usually plans a week in advance, carefully determining how many people will be served on a given day and what's the most economical, yet fulfilling way to feed them.

The Artist – The artist is very concerned with the visual appeal of each menu, and creates all meals with visual and textural variety. One minute they might be trussing a rack of lamb to resemble a crown, and in the next minute placing bravura splashes of colorful julienne squashes, peppers and carrots on the plate like an abstract painter.

The Nutritionist – The nutritionist seeks to satisfy nutritional needs of each diner with his or her well-planned menus. He or she makes sure that you receive elements of all the major food groups.

The Free Spirit – This approach takes what the market has to offer on any given day, choosing the best and most unusual cuts of meat and fish, the freshest vegetables and the most aromatic spices. Then the chef's creativity and experience take over, creating new and stimulating masterpieces.

CHAPTER TWO

Kitchen Shortcuts

The Shortest Distance between
Failure and Success

Culinary Tricks That Guarantee Amazing Results

Cooking a gourmet meal is like conducting a great symphony orchestra. Everything must happen at just the right moment and with just the right amount of emphasis. If the woodwind section comes in a moment too late or the percussion section is too strident, the symphony is ruined. Likewise, if the fish course is too dry or the hollandaise is runny, what should have been a gourmet feast will be nothing more than an expensive supper.

The kitchen of a four-star restaurant must prepare hundreds of meals in an evening, and the reputation of the restaurant rides on every dish, from lowly consomme to spectacular flaming dessert. So, how do master chefs manage to orchestrate all those meals night after night, and keep all their customers satisfied?

Is it all the years of rigorous training, or having the finest equipment at one's disposal? Or is it having a large and capable staff of sous chefs, pastry chefs, and apprentices? Master chefs will tell you that all of these are important, but the most important element is the proper use of time, because it is the one ingredient that is always in short supply.

Where great chefs differ from the rest of us is that they know secrets for making more of this precious commodity. And after you read Kitchen Shortcuts, you too will know how to make time work for you, instead of against you.

Flawless Fish, Poultry and Beef

Cauling the Immortal Bard

If you are a dedicated low-fat, low-cholesterol, low-calorie cook, avert your eyes. This entry is not for you. If you are willing to sacrifice some of the advantages of lean meat for a dramatic increase in flavor—read on!

Have your butcher supply you with thin strips of fatback, also called "bard" or "bardes," to wrap around the outside of a lean cut of meat such as a fillet of beef. Cover the entire cut of meat—top, bottom and sides—with the bard and then tie the bard in position with string before roasting.

Another technique is to wrap a roast with caul fat, which must also be ordered from your friend the butcher. Caul fat is a thin membrane from a pig's stomach prized for its lacy webbing of fat. After seasoning the roast, you completely encase the meat in the caul and tie with string before placing in the oven.

Freezing Cooked Chicken Breasts in Sauce

Cooked chicken breasts freeze well in sauces, but there is a danger of them becoming stringy and tough. To avoid this, cook the chicken breasts until they're slightly less than done, and freeze them. When they are frozen, add the sauce that's at room temperature and refreeze. On reheating, the chicken will finish cooking and the flavors of the sauce will integrate themselves into the meat. The alternative is to freeze the sauce and the chicken separately, reheat them separately and then finish in a microwave oven for 30 to 45 seconds.

Haul away, Joe—Testing Boiled Meats for Doneness

It's very difficult to determine the doneness of a piece of meat or chicken that's being poached or boiled. The size makes it hard to move around and the liquid gets in the way of seeing what's happening. An old French trick is to tie a piece of string around the meat and leave it dangling over the side of the cooking pot. Pull the string until the meat surfaces, and then test it.

Nothing Fishy about This

All a professional chef needs to do in order to determine how long to cook any kind of fish—steamed, poached, fried, grilled or broiled—is to measure it at its thickest point. He knows that it will take 10 minutes per inch. If there are any absolutes in life, this may be one of them.

A Foolproof Way to Marinate Meats

Self-sealing bags come in a large variety of sizes and they're perfect for marinating large pieces of meat or chicken. To insure even coverage, all you have to do is shake the bag. The bag takes up much less room in the refrigerator than a covered bowl. The best part is, the cleanup is a snap.

Butterflying Shrimp for Fun and Profit

Many seafood recipes call for butterflied shrimp. Here's how to do it:

1. Peel and devein shrimp.
2. With a small sharp knife, slice down the back of shrimp, cutting almost completely through.
3. Spread and flatten to form a butterfly shape.

Making the Bacon Last

If you cook bacon only occasionally, separate the strips, fold them in half and wrap them individually. Put everything in the freezer and you'll have your bacon a strip at a time.

Aw Shucks—
Opening Pesky Shellfish

Fresh oysters and clams are much easier to open after they've been left for an hour in the freezer.

Fasta Pasta

An Efficiency Primer

The only real shortcut to making perfect pasta is to do it right the first time. Cook pasta in a large pot of boiling, salted water, with a tablespoon of olive oil added to keep the pasta from sticking together. Watch the time and test for doneness as it cooks. The actual cooking time starts when the water returns to a full boil after adding the pasta.

* Dry pasta takes longer to cook than fresh. Begin testing after it has cooked for 5-6 minutes, depending on the shape and size. Fresh pasta may take no longer than 2-3 minutes.
* For hot pasta dishes, rinse just-cooked pasta under warm water to remove

CHEF'S BONUS

Here's a basic recipe for a simple tomato sauce that can't be beat for freshness and good taste.

BASIC FRESH TOMATO SAUCE FOR 4

1/3 cup olive oil
1 onion, peeled and chopped
Chopped fresh garlic to taste
1 3/4 pounds of fresh plum tomatoes prepared
  as described on the next page
2 tablespoons chopped fresh basil
Salt and pepper to taste
14 oz. spaghetti

Heat the olive oil in a heavy pan. Add the onion and garlic and fry gently for 5 minutes. Add the tomatoes, basil, salt and pepper and cook very gently for 30 minutes. Longer cooking will cause the tomatoes to break down, release liquid and make the sauce soupy.

Meanwhile, cook the pasta in plenty of boiling water, following the directions, until it's *al dente*. Drain thoroughly and place in a warmed serving dish. Pour the sauce over the top. Garnish with whole fresh basil leaves and serve immediately with a good grating cheese on the side.

starch, and to stop the cooking. But remember, a bit of starch holds the sauce, so don't get carried away. Pasta is best when drained and served with sauce immediately.

★ For the best flavor, toss pasta salads with a vinaigrette-style dressing while the pasta is still warm.

★ Large pieces of cheese will keep a long time when tightly wrapped; grated cheese won't. So keep a block of cheese handy, and grate it just before serving.

★ Use a large bowl, so the pasta and sauce have room to blend.

Perfect Plum Tomatoes, Perfectly Prepared, Make Perfect Sauces

When plum tomatoes are in season, ripe and beguiling, it's time to make fresh sauces for pastas, fish and side dishes. But even the best tomatoes can have tough peels and bitter seeds that can ruin the flavor and texture of an otherwise perfect sauce.

Here's a step-by-step look at peeling and seeding tomatoes for sauces.

COOKING TIP #7 FROM THE CHEFS

PEARLS OF WISDOM

To peel small white onions with a minimum of fuss, boil them in their skins for 45 seconds or so. After allowing them to drain, trim off their ends and their skins will slide off easily.

1. Select the ripest produce you can find.
2. Bring a pan of water to a boil.
3. Using a sharp knife, cut a shallow x through the skin at the bottom of each tomato.
4. Blanch batches of the tomatoes by placing them in the boiling water just long enough for the skin to soften but not for the tomatoes to begin cooking (about 60 seconds). Place them in a bowl of cold water to stop the cooking process.
5. You will see that the cut edges have begun to peel. Grasp the edge of the peel between your thumb and the flat of a knife blade

and pull the skin off in sections.

6. Remove the core and cut the tomatoes in half crosswise—around the middle, not from top to bottom. The seeds will easily come out of the chambers.

7. Dice the meat of the tomato with a good sharp knife to the desired size and use for sauces, salsas or garnish.

It's worth the effort!

Basics for a Basic Food Group

Keeping the Green Ones Green

There are several methods for keeping green vegetables green during the cooking process. One technique is to undercook them slightly in lightly salted water, then drop immediately into cold water to stop the cooking process. Reheat gently just before serving. Another trick: add a tablespoon of peanut oil to every 2 or 3 quarts of cooking water. The oil preserves the bright green color nicely.

There's No Such Thing as Leftover Parsley

Don't throw out parsley stems or, for that

COOKING TIP #8 FROM THE CHEFS

How to Make Quick Croutons

Add a gourmet touch to your salad while making use of day-old bread.

Cut 3 slices of bread into 1/2-inch cubes. In a medium skillet, heat 3 tablespoons of oil with 1/4 teaspoon of garlic powder. Cook the bread cubes, stirring frequently until they are crisp and golden. Drain well on paper towels.

Makes about 1 1/2 cups of croutons.

matter, celery leaves or asparagus and broccoli stalks. Collect all your vegetable trimmings in resealable storage bags and freeze. Add them to soups, stews, and sauces for a real flavor boost. The same goes for the water that vegetables have cooked in. Save and reuse it as a stock. It's full of flavor and nutrients.

COOKING TIP #9 FROM THE CHEFS

THE CONTAINER'S THE KEY TO QUICK MEALS

Invest in dishes with covers that can go directly from the freezer to the oven to the table. It saves time both in preparation and in cleanup.

Weep No More, My Lady— Chopping Onions without Tears

No, this tip does not require you to hold a piece of bread in your mouth like a greedy duck in the park. The true key to no-tears chopping is speed. First you slice a peeled onion into halves, cutting through the root end. Next, place the sliced side of the onion on a chopping board and slice down lengthwise through the onion half, taking care not to slice through the root. Then, holding the top of the onion half with one hand, make horizontal slices—parallel to the cutting board. Once again, you must be careful not to cut through the root. Finally, slice through the onion half from the top, instantly creating onion dice. For finely diced onions, make sure the slices are close together.

Two Easy Ways to Peel Roasted Peppers

Whether you roast peppers over a gas flame or under the broiler, you're left with the time-consuming and messy job of peeling off the charred skin. Expert chefs have devised a couple of ways to make this job quicker and easier. The first technique is to immediately plunge the roasted pepper into a bowl of ice water. This stops the cooking immediately and allows you to peel off the skin easily. The second technique is to place the roasted pepper in a plastic bag and close it up tightly for 15 minutes. As the pepper cools, the moisture is retained within the pepper, helping to loosen the charred skin. Remove the skin from the pepper. Slit it to open; wash out seeds and remove the veins.

Speedy Baked Potatoes

Potatoes will bake in a hurry if a thin slice is cut from each end and they are boiled in salted water for 10 minutes before popping into a very hot oven. The fastest method is 7 to 10 minutes in a microwave oven.

A leftover baked potato can be rebaked if you dip it in water and then bake in a 350-degree oven for 20 minutes.

Peeling Potatoes

Potatoes are easily peeled after cooking if you score them lightly before adding them to the water. When the potatoes are done, simply spear them with a fork and peel at the scored line. When you're dicing potatoes, drop them into cold water to prevent discoloring. Chopped vegetables fare best in non-metallic cups and bowls.

Anticipation and Organization

The One-Two Punch of the Professional Chef

The two most important secrets to making good use of your cooking time are not shortcuts in the classical sense of the word, but rather attitudes about cooking. As we saw in the last section, master chefs spend a great deal of time organizing their kitchens so that they can place their hands on the right kitchen implement when they need it. This eliminates the unnecessary steps and frantic rummaging through drawers that can be the downfall of the amateur cook.

Master chefs place a premium on planning ahead. They make sure that they have the right ingredients on hand for the next day's menu, and prepare portions of certain dishes in advance when possible. Here's an example of how you might put this principle to work. Let's say you are planning to serve your guests a lovely broiled flounder with a beurre bercy—a butter sauce made with shallots and white wine. Earlier in the day you might take a few minutes to chop your shallots and any other seasoning vegetables such as onion or parsley that your evening menu requires. Placed in a bowl and covered with plastic wrap, the chopped vegetables will still be in excellent shape when you need them in the evening. Most importantly, however, you will have just saved yourself 5 or 10 minutes for when you'll need them the most.

Get the Salad out of the Way Early

Mix the dressing in the bottom of your salad bowl, then crisscross the serving utensils in the bowl. Add the salad mixings, using the salad forks to help keep the bulk of them above the dressing. Cover with damp paper towels and chill in the refrigerator. Bring to room temperature when ready to serve, and toss.

Convenience Foods as Acceptable Shortcuts

In years past, the idea of a gourmet chef using prepared or "store-bought" foods in the home kitchen was akin to betraying one's country, a matter for shame and even culinary banishment. But times have changed, and so has the quality of prepared and convenience foods. When time is of the essence, it's great to have a pantry stocked with canned, bottled or freeze-dried foods to which you can add your own special touch. Supermarkets also offer prewashed leafy vegetables, premixed salad fixings, presliced vegetables of all types, and precut meats and fish. Even the bakeries are getting better. All of this is a bonanza to pressured cooks who are willing to use their skills to blend "homemade" with "store-bought" and still create a special meal.

Keep Stocks in Stock

Unless you're someone who has the time and space to make your own stocks for cooking, keep a supply of low-sodium canned beef and chicken broth on hand. They're essential for quick preparation of sauces and soups and can turn an impromptu supper into something special.

Bottled clam juice is a quick substitute for a fish stock. Remember, however, that it is high in salt. Adjust seasonings accordingly.

It's Not a Leftover—It's a Concept

When you plan the menus for your family, plan some of the meals with leftovers specifically in mind. With a little respicing and a different presentation, a beef stew can reappear as a curry over rice the following week.

Fixings for Emergency Meals—Keep Some in the Pantry

Maybe it was one of those days when you couldn't get to the store. Maybe company showed up unexpectedly. Expect the unexpected, and keep a separate stash of ingredients like pastas and sauces available for emergencies.

Thinking Ahead—Cooking Extra Rice and Pasta

Cook enough rice or pasta to last for the week's menus. They'll both store well in self-sealing plastic bags. Rice can also be cooked in quantity and frozen in serving sizes that will reheat quickly in the microwave.

The Beauty of Squeeze Bottles—A Real Chef's Secret

Those inexpensive plastic squeeze bottles used in the home primarily for ketchup and mustard have a much more glorified role and are real time-savers in the professional kitchen. Chefs use them to hold sauces, cooking oils, honey and syrups and anything else they can think of to fill them. Why? The bottles control the mess, allow for fast and accurate measurement, are easy to hold and store conveniently.

"X" Marks the Spot

If you take a pencil and mark an "X" on your hard-boiled eggs before storing them in the refrigerator, you won't have to waste time sorting them out from the fresh ones.

Collecting Leftover Wine for Cooking

Wines left over from dinner parties may not be drinkable after a few days but they are useful for sauces and enhancing salad dressings for quite some time. Gather what's left in the bottles, store in a bottle that can be tightly sealed, and keep it handy in the kitchen.

Saving a Step While Squeezing a Lemon

When you add any citrus juice to a recipe, wrap the fruit in cheesecloth and squeeze it directly into the bowl or pot. The seeds will be trapped in the cheesecloth and you'll have one less dish to wash.

It Doesn't Have to be the Pits

To pit olives in a flash, lay them out on your work surface and give them a few turns of your rolling pin. The pits will be easily removed and the flesh will be laid out for easy chopping.

Hold the Salt!

Wait until the water comes to a boil before adding salt. Why? Salted water has a higher boiling point, so if you add it too early you only add to the boiling time.

Maybe It's Just a Little Grating

If you need a small amount of a hard cheese like Parmesan or Romano, use a lemon zester instead of dragging out the cheese grater.

It's up to You, Honey

Honey is a professional chef's secret weapon. Most kitchens stock several different blends of different strengths. It keeps indefinitely and works in hundreds of sauces, glazes and syrups. It goes beautifully with fish such as salmon and meats such as chicken and lamb. It can often be used as a substitute for sugar.

If a recipe calls for a pronounced honey flavor, look for one with the darkest color—it means the taste will be strong. If you're looking for something silky and sweet for a muffin or fresh-baked bread, look for the lightest color available.

Restoring Frozen Flavors

Freezing foods, while convenient, tends to dilute their strength and cause a significant loss of flavor. After you've thawed a dish and it's been fully reheated, taste and correct the seasonings before serving.

Nonstick Measuring for Sticky Things

Measure syrups, molasses and honey—and anything that's sticky, for that matter—in lightly greased cups, rinsed in warm water. Add the sticky stuff to the rest of the ingredients with a rubber spatula.

Taking the Measure of Baking Pans

Recipes usually specify a certain size baking pan, and success often depends on using it. If your baking pans don't have the measurements stamped on the bottom, measure the length, width and depth to see if they're what's called for. To determine the volume in cups or quarts, measure the amount of water it takes to fill the pan.

Put That Spatula Back on the Hook—Flip Your Food

The fastest way to flip small pieces of food in a frying pan is to shake the pan to loosen them and flip them with a quick downward jerk. It's easy to do and you can practice with a couple of small bean bags until you get the hang of it.

Quick and Clean—Melting Butter and Chocolate in the Microwave

Place chocolate or butter in self-sealing bags and microwave it until it reaches the desired consistency.

Counter Measures—Keeping Wax Paper in Place

To hold wax paper to the countertop when rolling dough or grating foods, dampen the counter before placing the paper on it.

COOKING TIP #10

A POTPOURRI OF HELPFUL HINTS

- A kitchen whisk works just as well as a sifter for mixing dry ingredients. Do it right in the bowl.
- Ripen green fruits by placing them in a perforated plastic bag. The holes allow air movement, yet retain the odorless gas the fruits produce to promote ripening.
- If you're entertaining and really pressed for time, set the table and decorate the dining room the day before.
- In a pinch, an egg slicer will do a good job slicing mushrooms.
- To quickly ripen garden tomatoes or avocados, put them in a brown paper bag. Close the bag and leave at room temperature for a few days. Putting an apple in the bag can also hasten the ripening process.
- When pan frying, heat the pan before adding butter or oil.

FROM THE CHEFS

- Boil vinegar in a new frying pan to prevent foods from sticking to it.
- A cup of water or a piece of bread added to the bottom portion of a broiler pan helps absorb smoke and grease.
- A few teaspoons of sugar and cinnamon slowly burned on top of the stove will hide unpleasant cooking odors.
- Grate a stick of butter to soften it quickly.
- Soften butter for spreading by inverting a small heated pan over the butter dish for a few moments.
- Dip measuring spoons or cups into hot water before measuring shortening or butter. The fat will slip out easily without sticking.
- If you wet the dish on which the gelatin is to be unmolded, you can move the gelatin until it's centered.

Use wax paper on the counter when you're peeling and chopping vegetables. When you're finished, wrap up the paper and toss the waste away.

Neatness Counts—Bag Those Nuts and Crumbs

To make bread or cracker crumbs without making a mess, put them in a plastic bag and roll with a rolling pin, or put them in a blender. You can do the same thing with nuts.

No Spills or Tipovers Necessary When Filling Molds

To fill odd-shaped molds or ramekins that could tip easily, place them in a muffin tin before pouring. To fill them, use a narrow-mouthed pitcher.

A Firm but Salty Grip on Things

Slippery food is easier to hold if you dip your fingertips in a little salt.

Brighter Brights

Adding a little lemon to red cabbage and beets will keep the colors bright.

Keep the Plastic Wrap in Cold Storage

You won't drive yourself insane trying to get a piece of plastic wrap off the roll if you keep the box in the refrigerator.

A Quick Fix for Souring Milk

No matter how careful and efficient you are, there will be a time when you reach into the refrigerator for a cup of milk and discover that it's just started to turn. Baking soda can save the day. Add 2 teaspoons, mix it in and you'll be able to use the milk in recipes.

COOKING TIP #11 FROM THE CHEFS

SCISSORS WILL...

- cut pizza more effectively than a knife.
- trim the overhanging pastry on a pie with ease.
- make mincemeat of fresh herbs.
- break up whole tomatoes right in the can.

Saving Energy Can Mean Saving Time—Make Your Stove Work for You

★ Use pots and pans with flat bottoms to keep the burner heat from escaping. Always use a pan the same size as the burner.

★ Make sure the reflector pans beneath your stove's heating elements are bright and clean. Shiny reflector pans help focus heat rays on the bottom of cooking utensils.

★ Use tightly fitting lids. Food in covered

pans begins boiling or steaming quicker and lets you use lower temperature settings.

★ Use a microwave oven whenever possible for precooking and prep. It will use less than half the power of a conventional oven, and cook the food in about one-fourth the time.

★ Use the minimum amount of liquid called for in the recipe. Most frozen or fresh vegetables can be cooked in no more than 1/4 cup of water. Even eggs will boil in 1/4 cup of water if the pan has a tightly fitting lid.

★ On the stove top, start with high heat and lower the setting when the food starts to bubble or boil.

★ In an oven, cook as many dishes at one time as you can. Foods with cooking temperatures within 25 degrees can be cooked simultaneously at the same temperature.

★ Preheat your oven only when necessary. Many foods do not require it.

★ Don't peek. Each time the oven door is opened the temperature drops 25 to 50 degrees.

Hot Off the Grill

Cleanup is easier if you coat the grill top with vegetable cooking spray before barbecuing.

If you use a charcoal grill, remember that a fire is ready for cooking when the coals are covered with gray ash—about 20 to 30 minutes after lighting.

Toss damp hickory chunks, outer onion layers or garlic halves on hot coals for flavorful meats, poultry and fish. Grated orange and lemon peel add a light touch to fruits and vegetables.

Quick, Delicious Fruit Sorbet

Nothing tops off a meal or cleanses the palate quite as nicely as a fruit sorbet. Now there's a way you can make them in a matter of minutes. The technique calls for freezing cans of fruit in their heavy syrup for a minimum of 12 hours. Once properly frozen, place the can in hot water for roughly 1 minute. This will allow you to slide the fruit out easily once the can is opened. After you remove the fruit from the can, chop it into small pieces approximately 1-inch square and feed into the food processor. For additional flavor, you can add frozen yogurt and/or your favorite fruit cordial.

Fast Facts about Radishes

Radishes are a versatile and delicious vegetable and are often overlooked as a viable and quick addition to a meal. Here are some tips for including them on a hurry-up menu.

★ For an unusual vegetable side dish, sauté quartered radishes in butter until crisp but tender—about 2 minutes. Sprinkle with cracked black pepper and serve.

★ Stir chopped or sliced radishes into tuna, egg, potato or chicken salad.

★ Thinly sliced radishes make a tasty, fresh garnish sprinkled over New England clam chowder or other milk-based soups.

★ For extra crunch and bite, add sliced

radishes to stir-fry.

★ Stir chopped radishes into plain yogurt or sour cream as a topping for baked potatoes or chili.

★ Bagels spread with cream cheese and sliced radishes make a quick appetizer or snack.

★ Roast radish halves by brushing with oil in a 450-degree oven. They go well with roast beef or chicken.

★ A combination of mayonnaise and chopped radishes makes a tangy instant spread for ham or roast beef sandwiches.

★ Thinly slivered radishes stirred into rice pilaf add an unexpected nip and crunch.

When in Rome, Do as the French Do

Translating Those Foreign Recipes

The more you cook, the more likely you are to run into some great European cookbooks that haven't been Americanized. The measurements will be in liters, grams and other units that are a little unfamiliar.

The metric system is a way of measuring based on the decimal system with larger measures being subdivided into units of ten. Food researchers and European cooks have always used the metric system because it is more precise than American weights and measures. You'll find that the big difference in recipes is that dry ingredients like flour and sugar are weighed rather than measured in a cup. Meats, fruits and vegetables will be sold by the kilogram instead of the pound and will be asked for by weight rather than by cup no matter how they are prepared for the recipe, for instance sliced, diced or chopped. Small measurements like teaspoons and tablespoons will not be likely to change.

Liquids are measured in measuring cups, but the calibrations are marked in liters, 1/2 liters, 1/4 liters and milliliters instead of cups, 1/2 cups and so on.

Metric Equivalents for U.S. Measurements

U.S. MEASURE	METRIC EQUIVALENT
1/8 teaspoon (t.)	0.5 milliliter (ml.)
1/4 t.	1 ml.
1/2 t.	2 ml.
1 t.	5 ml.
1/2 tablespoon (T.)	7 ml.
1 T. (3 teaspoons)	15 ml.

2 T. (1 fluid ounce)	30 ml.
1/4 cup (c.)(2 fluid ounces)	60 ml.
1/3 c.	80 ml.
1/2 c. (4 fluid ounces)	125 ml.
2/3 c.	160 ml.
3/4 c. (6 fluid ounces)	180 ml.
1 c. (8 fluid ounces)	250 ml.
1 pint (2 cups)	500 ml.
1 quart (4 cups)	1 Liter

Metric Equivalents for Temperatures

FAHRENHEIT	CELSIUS
200 F.	100 C.
250 F.	120 C.
275 F.	140 C.
300 F.	150 C.
325 F.	160 C.
350 F.	180 C.
375 F.	190 C.
400 F.	200 C.
425 F.	220 C.
450 F.	230 C.

Metric Equivalents for Weight

U.S. MEASURE	METRIC EQUIVALENT
1/2 ounce (oz.)	15 grams (gm.)
1 oz.	30 gm.
2 oz.	60 gm.
3 oz.	85 gm.
1/4 lb. (4 oz.)	115 gm.
1/2 lb. (8 oz.)	225 gm.
3/4 lb. (12 oz.)	340 gm.
1 lb. (16 oz.)	450 gm.

NOTE: All metric equivalents are approximate; they have been rounded to the nearest metric equivalent for ease of use.

CHAPTER THREE

Presentation Secrets

Getting the Right Look

A Great Tasting Meal Should Look Great, Too

It is one of the ironies of cooking that even the most special meal is gone with a few flashes of knife and fork. The dinner that took hours to prepare is over and only the dishes remain. That's why cooking is such a labor of love. A great meal is a gift from the cook to those who share it. Its purpose is not only to nourish and sustain, but to add a little pleasure and beauty to the lives of those at the dinner table. The care a cook takes in the making and presentation of the "daily bread" is all about the quality of life and a celebration of the bounty of nature.

Great chefs and dedicated amateurs know that good food should be a feast for the eyes as well as the palate. A big part of their artistry is discovering unique and interesting ways to combine and present the food. Balance and harmony of texture, flavor and color excite the imagination and stimulate the appetite.

Attitudes about food and dining have changed dramatically over the last 20 years. Fine dining and good presentation are no longer only for the rich. Not only do people want to eat well, they want to appreciate what they're eating and enjoy the pleasure of a beautiful plate and a beautiful table.

Three Steps for Presenting a Special Meal

1. Create a menu that allows for foods that contrast in color, shape and texture. When planning a meal, try to visualize how each course will look on the plate

and how the basic elements will combine to create a pleasing picture.

2. Create a table setting that complements and enhances the menu. In the best of all possible worlds, the plates, glasses and silver reflect what is being served. But you don't have to have the perfect china and silver. Use your imagination and what's around the house to add special decorative touches. For instance, you might try making a centerpiece of tiny children's toys and flowers for a birthday party or baby shower.

3. Create an atmosphere that unifies and focuses the presentation. Whether you're eating in the dining room, the kitchen or the backyard, make use of candles and centerpieces of fruits, vegetables or flowers that say the meal is special.

Research, Research, Research

Most great chefs will readily admit that they're always looking over each other's shoulders for new ways to send great meals to the table. They use everything they can get their hands on to come up with ways to make their presentations unique. Recipes may be closely guarded secrets, but it's hard to hide a beautifully designed plate. When you dine at a fine restaurant, take the time to look at what the chef has done to make your meal visually exciting. If you can't spend a lot of time in great restaurants, don't give up hope. Cookbooks and cooking magazines are also great sources of inspiration. They provide unique and exciting ideas for pleasing presentations. The pictures are loaded with innovations and concepts from the best cooks in the world. Study them carefully, collect notions that interest you and keep them in a journal or notebook to help you develop presentations of your own.

I Can't Believe It's Butter

Flavored or compound butters make a wonderful accompaniment to broiled meats. Consider mixing warm butter with any of the following: parsley, a mix of fresh herbs, tangy mustard, hot sauce, shallots or green onions, minced garlic or other flavorings. A small serving placed on the meat before bringing it to the table is an excellent garnish.

Flavored butters can do far more than add a touch of taste and color to a steak. They can become part of the whole presentation as well. Put flavored butter in tiny serving dishes and chill before placing on the table as a wonderfully edible decorative element.

Or create a butter log. Mince the ingredients, such as herbs, mix them well in softened butter and use plastic wrap to shape into a log. Refrigerate until just firm, then roll the log in a mixture of roughly chopped edible flowers such as roses, pansies, chive blossoms or dill. Chill the butter logs and slice into 1/4 to 1/2 inch rounds.

Join the Radish Fan Club

To make radish fans, start with large oval-shaped radishes. Trim the root ends and most of the leaves. Place each radish on a cutting surface and, with a thin sharp knife, make closely spaced, vertical cuts crosswise along the sides of the radish. Be very careful to not cut all the way through the root end. Chill, covered with ice water, for 30 minutes. Radish fans make a lovely garnish alongside roasts, grilled meats and Oriental dishes.

A Bouquet of Radish or Cherry Tomato Roses

Use medium-sized round radishes. Trim off the root ends, leaving small circles of white. Hold each radish, root side up, and cut a thin rounded slice on one side of the radish, leaving it attached at the base. Make three or four cuts, creating petals spaced evenly around the radish. Cut a second thin slice behind the original petals. Repeat around the radish. Drop in a bowl filled with iced water and chill for thirty minutes. Use radish roses to add color to meat and cheese trays, salads and sandwich plates. Also cut radish roses to serve on a platter of crudities with dip.

Use the same technique to cut cherry tomatoes and serve as either an elegant garnish or a side dish. Serve cold, or cook until tender in a double boiler with two tablespoons of butter and freshly chopped dill. The rich redness of the tomatoes and the green of the dill finish a platter of roast beef beautifully.

A Perfect Marriage—The Right Wine for the Right Meal

The first rule of choosing the right wine for the right food is a simple one: If you like it, drink it. Let your palate be the judge and combine any foods and wines that you enjoy. Over the years, however, certain foods and wines have consistently come together in successful unions. Here are some classic combinations.

★ Light, dry white wines (Chardonnay, Chablis, Riesling, Muscadet): Fish, shellfish, oysters, clams; cold meat and chicken dishes; egg dishes including omelets; light cheeses

★ Full-bodied white wines (White Burgundy, Cotes Du Rhone, Graves): Fish, poultry, veal, main dishes with cream sauces, pork, pates

★ Rosé wine: Goes with almost anything, but it's usually served with cold dishes, picnic fare, pates, eggs, and pork

★ Light-bodied to medium-bodied red wines (Bordeaux, Merlot, Pinot Noir): Roast chicken and all other roasted poultry, stews, veal, lamb, beef, pork, ham, liver, pate, cheeses

★ Full-bodied red wines (Burgundies, Rhones, Cabernet Sauvignon, Zinfandel): Strong-flavored meats and poultry such as duck, goose, roasts of beef, pork, strong cheeses

★ Champagne: Serve with almost any dish and throughout a meal.

Classic Combinations and Presentations from Chefs Who Know—The French

Certain combinations of entrées and the side dishes that accompany them have become classic. The French have spent centuries perfecting combinations that are pleasing not only to the palate but to the eye as well. Following are some classics that are worth considering when you plan a special menu. Use them as a springboard for creating classics of your own.

FISH

★ Julienne of carrots, onions, celery and mushrooms in butter sauce
★ Boiled potatoes and green beans
★ Steamed rice and sautéed mushrooms

ROAST CHICKEN

★ Broiled tomatoes and baked potatoes

★ Sweet green peas and mashed potatoes
★ Glazed carrots and glazed onions
★ Braised onions and risotto
★ Sautéed mushrooms and brussels sprouts

DUCK

★ Green peas and turnips
★ Pureed chestnuts and brussels sprouts
★ Red cabbage and parsley potatoes

BEEF STEAK

★ French fries and green peas
★ Baked potato and sautéed spinach
★ Stuffed mushrooms and artichoke hearts
★ Broiled mushrooms and parsley potatoes

VEAL ROAST

★ Risotto with mushrooms and

braised lettuce
★ Buttered noodles with glazed carrots and onions

LAMB

★ Sautéed spinach and white beans in tomato sauce
★ Rice with mushrooms and sweet peas
★ Stuffed tomatoes and green beans
★ Ratatouille and scalloped potatoes
★ Medley of spring vegetables—carrots, peas, turnips, onions, and green beans

PORK

★ Boiled potatoes and red cabbage
★ Garlic mashed potatoes and white cabbage
★ Brussels sprouts with cheese
★ Buttered potatoes and braised leeks
★ Fruit sauces (apple, cherry, peach) and boiled potatoes
★ Turnips and glazed onions

Don't Just Chop or Grate—Peel It!

Use your trusty vegetable peeler to slice paper-thin pieces of vegetables like mushrooms, cucumbers or carrots. Decorate salads and main dishes with the slices. Do the same thing with hard cheeses like Parmesan as a finishing touch for a pasta dish. You can also strip off spirals of the skin of citrus fruits and tomatoes. Twist them into flower shapes by wrapping the spirals around your finger in concentric circles. Use them as garnishes for dinner plates or serving platters.

Mold Side Dish Vegetables for a New Look

The many different styles, sizes and shapes of the metal molds designed for desserts or gelatins can create a whole new look at your table. Molded rice or leafy vegetables (like chopped, fully drained spinach) look terrific set directly on the dinner plate or serving platter. Spray the molds with a nonstick cooking spray and fill with your vegetable

COOKING TIP #12
FROM THE CHEFS

WARMING PLATES AND PLATTERS

A sure means of enhancing the elegance of a meal is to take the time to heat plates and serving platters in a low oven before using them. If you don't have room in the oven, place them in the dishwasher on the drying cycle.

of choice. Compact tightly. Unmold onto plates and garnish with sauces and herbs.

Individual Chocolate Cups
for a Stunning Dessert

Serving a dessert of sliced fresh fruit, pudding or ice cream in individual chocolate cups is the perfect ending to an elegant meal. And it's easy to do. Melt bittersweet chocolate in a double boiler. Using a fine pastry brush, paint the inside of paper muffin cups with chocolate.

COOKING TIP #13 FROM THE CHEFS

CLEAN CUTS THE PRO'S WAY

If you spend the time and effort to make a perfect cheesecake or other cream-based dessert, it's important that you present it perfectly. Cheesecake and its kin are notoriously difficult to cut without jagged edges or crumpled points. Professional chefs always cut delicate cakes with a flat, thin-bladed knife. But that's just part of it. Professional chefs advise using a warm blade. Either run the knife under very warm water or through an open flame between slices. In either event, wipe the blade after each cut. If you'd like a lower-tech solution, cut the cake with unflavored dental floss stretched tightly between your fingers.

Chill them in the freezer until they're firm and you're ready to serve. Remove the paper, fill the molds and serve on a chilled plate with an appropriate fruit sauce puddled on the plate. Garnish with a sprig of mint. For an extra touch, use a vegetable peeler to shave ribbons of white chocolate onto the dish. Sprinkle lightly with powdered sugar if desired.

Beautiful Pasta Presentations— Matching Shapes

Take a look at the pasta dishes in a good Italian restaurant. Notice that the shapes of the ingredients tend to match the shapes of the pasta. As a general rule, the vegetables for linguine are cut into thin strips (or julienned). Chunkier vegetables, like broccoli, are cut into florets and used with shells or spiral-shaped fusilli. This not only enhances the look of the dish but makes it easier to eat. Incidentally, pastas with ribs or indentations are used in thin sauces to help "hold" the sauce. Smooth pastas are used in thicker sauces that cling more easily to the exterior.

It's Not Just Parsley Anymore— Garnishes are Everywhere

Fresh vegetables, herbs and flowers make perfect accents and add that professional touch to a plate. Sprinkle chopped chives, scallions, tarragon or dill around the dish. Julienne red and yellow peppers and criss-cross them over the entrée. Serve tiny vegetables, like baby carrots complete with tops. New yellow squash or cherry tomatoes can be blanched and served whole to create a wonderful palette of edible color and contrast. Whole sprigs of rosemary, thyme, chervil, tarragon, cilantro or scallion complement the seasoning in a dish and add a beauty and fragrance sure to thrill your guests. Edible flowers such as nasturtiums or pansies make elegant contributions to the visual feast.

Any fresh herb, vegetable or edible flower is a potential garnish. You're limited only by your imagination. Choose fresh herbs that complement the spices in the meal.

COOKING TIP #14 FROM THE CHEFS

PASTA SALADS CAN'T FAIL

Pasta is one of the world's most universal bases for beautiful-looking dishes—especially salads. Almost any combination of ingredients can be mixed with the chunkier pastas such as ziti, fusilli and rigatoni. The result will be not only delicious but serve as a centerpiece for a buffet dinner or a simple lunch.

Colored Pastas Add Pleasing Contrast to the Table—Get out of the Two-Color Rut

Not so long ago there were two basic pasta colors available to the home cook: white and green. The only way to add variety and color was to make fresh pasta at home. Now the markets are stocked with colored pastas that run the entire spectrum of the rainbow.

They've become an important element in professional menu design.

Dusting—The Final Confectioner's Touch

Desserts are often "finished" in the professional kitchen with a dusting of confectioner's sugar. It adds a little sweetness and the color accentuates that of the final product. But it doesn't have to end there. Try dusting with cocoa, cinnamon or nutmeg as a substitute or in combination with the sugar. A final touch might be a dusting of finely ground almonds, walnuts or hazelnuts. Dust sprigs of mint or edible leaves to enhance them as a garnish.

Chefs also create dusting patterns on cakes and pastries by sifting the sugar through special paper doilies available at commercial outlets. You can make your own using manila file folders or another kind of heavy paper. Trace your design and then cut it out with a razor knife.

Painting with Sauces— Another Use for Squeeze Bottles

The squeeze bottle isn't just for ketchup and mustard. Professionals use them to decorate both main course and dessert plates with sauces of contrasting colors and flavors. Fill one bottle with the main sauce and another with a contrasting sauce. Follow your instincts to create unusual and interesting patterns on the plate. One technique is to take the primary sauce and cover the bottom of the plate, then squeeze the second sauce in concentric circles. As an added touch, take the tip of a knife and draw it gently through the circles creating a series of waves. Your instinct, imagination and some experimentation offer endless possibilities.

Designer Soups

A plain old pureed cream of potato soup will quickly become a visual treat with the addition of a contrasting puree of broccoli floating on the top. The key is to make sure that the decorative addition is pureed to the same consistency as the base. If it's heavier, it will sink to the bottom. Skate gently across the puree with a spoon to create a pattern. Once you've created the pattern, add a garnish of chopped spices or sprigs of fresh herbs.

Straight from the Pizza Parlor— How to Puddle a Sauce on a Dinner Plate

It's a tradition in most homes to fill the plate with food and then spoon on the gravy. While that's fine for a turkey dinner, professional cooks often spread the sauce for a dish on the plate before dishing up the entrée and side dishes. The key is the same trick used at the pizzeria to spread tomato sauce on the dough. Simply ladle the sauce into the center of the plate. Then take the bowl of the ladle, and starting in the center, spread the sauce to the plate rim with a brisk circular motion.

Go Vertical for a Change

People generally arrange their food in "compartments"—the lamb chop next to the rice, the rice next to the peas, and so on. Next time you are in an upscale restaurant notice that often the chef has made a mountain of his meal. You can, too. Mound the main side dish—whether it's potatoes or rice or vegetables—in the center of the plate. Then prop your entrée against it in an interesting pattern. Add the remaining sauces, sides and garnishes. Chops, chicken breasts, and fish fillets adapt themselves perfectly for this technique and you'll be pleased with the elegant results.

Deep-Fried Parsley— Different but Good

For a unique accent to chicken or fish, try deep-frying fresh parsley in very hot oil for a few seconds. Drain on paper towels and use as a distinctive garnish. Just be sure the oil is fresh and unflavored by that last batch of French fries.

Jazzing up the Festive Punch Bowl

You won't have to worry about ice diluting the punch if you freeze some of the punch in a decorative mold and put it in the punch bowl. If you want to add pieces of fruit to the mold, wait until the punch is partially frozen but still slushy. Add colorful accents by freezing pieces of fruit or sprigs of mint in ice cube trays with the punch. Add to the punch as necessary.

Frosted Grapes— Sweets to the Sweet

Frosted red and green grapes are a wonderful addition to the dessert plate. The key— brush them with a lightly beaten egg white, and dip them in confectioner's sugar. Try this with cherries, too.

Bacon Curls—Crisp and Pretty

Crisp curled bacon is a traditional garnish for many hearty winter meals. Use it to add a new look to breakfast plates, as well. Fry the bacon until just limp and then wrap it around the tines of a fork. Continue to fry with the bacon wrapped around the fork until it's crisp. Remove and then drain.

Fluted Mushrooms—
An Elegant Touch

Before sautéing medium-sized mushrooms, cut a fluted spiral in the cap with a sharp paring knife. First, wash the mushroom and remove the stem. Hold the mushroom in one hand, and a paring knife rigidly in the other. Make the fluted cuts by turning the mushroom into the stationary knife. Rotate the mushroom so the cut travels from crown to bottom, and completely around the cap.

Onion Chrysanthemums—
A Savory Bouquet

Small- to medium-sized white onions can become beautiful flowers that decorate a platter of pot roast or a baked chicken.

First, peel the onions without cutting off the ends. Then take a sharp knife and slice as if you were cutting wedges out of an orange. Make the cuts 1/8 to 1/4 inch apart, and cut only about 3/4 of the way down to the root end. Hold the onion under warm running water and gently spread the sections away from the center to make "petals". Although they are quite beautiful as is, you can also tint them with food coloring to further the flower effect.

Another alternative is to leave a small bulb in the center which can be left as is, or cut out and replaced with a radish rosette, a cherry tomato or a cluster of black olives.

Swabbing the Deck

Just like anything else, excellent presentation is in the details. Dribbles of sauce or juice on the edge of the plate ruins the effect you've worked so hard to achieve. They're also an inevitable part of the process—even for the pros. Chefs keep a warm damp towel close by and simply wipe the mistakes away before sending the plate out of the kitchen. For those tiny little smidgens, a cotton swab or piece of rolled up cheesecloth is the perfect solution.

Nuts to That!—Sifting for Consistency

There are a great number of desserts that call for toppings of grated nuts. Sometimes it's difficult to chop everything to a consistent size—which can be very important for the finished look. A simple solution is to sift the chopped nuts through the wire mesh of a flour sifter or strainer. Pieces of the same size will fall through and the larger chunks will remain on top. Use either what's left, or what went through, depending on the size you need.

Skewers That Don't Burn

If you are serving meats or vegetables on bamboo skewers, the charred-wood look spoils the effect. Soak the skewers in water for several hours before skewering and they won't burn.

Leaf Nothing to Chance

Large leafed lettuces, like romaine, are perfect for lining serving platters to hold cold entrées like salads and poached fish. Create a bed of leaves around the edge of the platter or bowl, and fill the center with the main dish. Garnish with slices of lemon, cucumber, sliced tomatoes, red onions or whatever strikes your fancy.

Look for packages of oversized grape leaves in cooking supply or specialty food stores. They make a perfect surface for presenting a mix of cheeses and fruit.

CHAPTER FOUR

Healthy Substitutions

Lighten Up

Less Fat, More Taste

When most people think of master chefs, they conjure up images of overweight men decked out in chefs' hats and white uniforms. Although the familiar chef's attire is still very much with us, today's chefs are just as concerned about health and fitness as the public at large.

Perhaps more importantly, they've realized that success depends on keeping your customers satisfied. And as our population grows older and more health conscious, more and more devotees of haute cuisine are asking for gourmet dishes prepared with less salt, less fat and less cholesterol.

In the last 20 years, this new emphasis on healthy eating has given rise to several important movements that are still influencing master chefs throughout the world. Notable among them are cuisine minceur and nouvelle cuisine. Both emphasize lighter menus with fewer red meats and more fish and poultry. They use more vegetables and lighter sauces, and serve smaller portions. Grilling is preferred over sautéing; and chefs delight in artful, colorful presentation.

Admittedly, it's a lot easier to prepare elaborate dishes that taste great than to make wonderful low-calorie entrees. When in doubt, all you have to do is sauté in rich creamery butter, or slather on a rich hollandaise sauce. But once you learn a few simple principles you, too, can prepare great-tasting, healthy meals.

In this section, you'll learn some of the tricks and techniques used by professional chefs to prepare lighter versions of your favorite dishes. Included are easy substitutions that let you make low-fat, low-calorie dishes without sacrificing the most important ingredient of all—taste.

Making Healthy Substitutions without Sacrificing Taste

Small changes in your favorite recipes can result in huge reductions in calories, salt, fat and cholesterol. The best way to begin is to study the dishes you like to make and look for ways to reduce offending ingredients while increasing fiber. Try some of the following suggestions. Chances are neither you nor your dinner guests will notice the difference in taste.

★ Bacon—Use Canadian bacon or baked ham, both of which are much leaner than regular bacon.
★ Butter—A good substitute for butter is polyunsaturated margarine or vegetable oil. One tablespoon of butter equals 1 tablespoon of margarine or 3/4 tablespoon of oil.
★ Eggs—There are several options. You

COOKING TIP #15 FROM THE CHEFS

SALT OF THE EARTH

You can cut down on the amount of salt you use if you add it when your dish is almost done. This is especially true in soups. By waiting until the end of the process, you season only the broth, creating a dish that tastes of more salt than is actually there.

can use cholesterol-free egg substitutes, which typically call for 1/4 cup of egg substitute for each egg. Or make your own substitute by mixing 1 egg white with 2 teaspoons of polyunsaturated oil for each egg. For baking, some experts maintain you can use two egg whites in place of each whole egg.

★ Pasta—For an occasional change from pasta, substitute spaghetti squash. When cooked, the long vegetable strands resemble linguini. Another technique is to cut zucchini into long julienne strips before steaming. Cover with a nice homemade tomato sauce and fresh Parmesan cheese for a delicious vegetable "pasta."

★ Chocolate—Substitute unsweetened cocoa powder blended with vegetable oil or margarine for the higher-fat chocolate squares called for in desserts.

★ Sweeteners—Instead of white sugar, many cooks use honey or fruit juices as sweeteners. If you substitute honey for sugar, you can reduce the amount of sweetener needed by approximately 25 percent without sacrificing taste or satisfaction. As a rule of thumb, some experts recommend cutting the sweetener called for by 30-50 percent in all recipes.

★ Salt—Salt is one of the more difficult tastes to replicate, but many cooks have successfully substituted various herbs such as marjoram, oregano, thyme, basil and rosemary, or spices such as cumin, chili powder, curry and paprika.

★ Shortening—When baking breads, you

can substitute vegetable oil for shortening to cut down on saturated fats. If you're making cookies or other sweetened baked goods, you can use soft margarine as a substitute. To cut down on calories as well as saturated fats, you can replace some of the margarine or oil with pureed fruit. Some cooks swear by apple butter. Applesauce seems to be a consensus favorite.

★ Wine—What you substitute for wine depends entirely upon the nature of the dish. For hot entrees, a mixture of 1 part lemon juice to 7 parts chicken stock works best. For desserts, substitute fruit juice for the chicken stock.

Get the Fat out of Salad Dressings

Salads are usually considered to be the dieter's best friend. Salad greens and other raw vegetables are blessedly low in calories and high in fiber and nutrients. So most people feel incredibly virtuous when they dig into a large salad.

Unfortunately, their good intentions are

often for naught because their salad dressing is loaded with fat and calories. Fortunately, professional chefs have devised a number of ways to make your favorite salad dressings less damaging to your waistline and heart.

First and foremost, you can reduce the amount of fat by replacing all or some of the vegetable oil with chicken or beef stock. The gelatin in the stock will lend enough thickness to the final dressing and help duplicate the texture of your old high-fat recipe.

In creamy recipes, such as ranch or Russian dressings, you can substantially cut fat by using low-fat sour cream. An even more effective calorie cutter is a sour cream substitute made by blending low-fat cottage cheese with a small amount of plain yogurt. If a recipe calls for mayonnaise, cut fat and calories by using a mixture of 50 percent mayo and 50 percent low-fat yogurt.

Dairy Products A Special Case

Because they're an integral part of so many recipes, and because some milk products are high in fat, substituting for dairy products is an important consideration. As you can see from the table below, the range of calories per cup in the varieties of milk alone is quite staggering. The good news is that you have a wide range of substitutions, depending on how much fat you want to cut in your total intake of calories.

Milk the Perfect Food?

MILK PRODUCT	CALORIES PER CUP
Skim milk, made from powdered milk	80
Skim milk	90 to 100
Low fat, 1% milk	100
Low fat, 2% nonfat milk solids	130
Whole milk	150
Half-and-half	300
Light cream	480
Heavy cream	800

Milk Product Substitutions

★ **Sour Cream**—There are a number of good ways to create low-fat sour cream. The simplest: run low-fat cottage cheese through a blender or food processor until it has the same consistency as sour cream. For additional flavor, some chefs add a couple of tablespoons of plain, low-fat yogurt.

Another terrific sour cream substitute is yogurt cheese, an easy-to-make versatile addition to your low-fat repertoire. Make it by forcing the moisture out of low-fat yogurt (see tip following page) and then refrigerating the solids overnight. With the addition of chives, yogurt cheese makes a great dressing on baked potatoes.

Yet another way to make a mock sour cream is by thinning low-fat ricotta cheese with yogurt. And finally, you can make a passable sour cream by whipping a can of cold evaporated skim milk to which you've added a teaspoon of lemon juice.

★ **Milk**—Add 2 tablespoons of vegetable

COOKING TIP #16 FROM THE CHEFS

Basic Recipe for Yogurt Cheese

Place a pint of plain (unflavored) low-fat yogurt in a bowl lined with four layers of cheesecloth. Gather up the corners of the cheesecloth and tie together with string. Place the cheesecloth in a strainer, and suspend it over the bowl in the refrigerator for roughly five hours, allowing the moisture from the yogurt to drip into the bowl. Place the contents of the cheesecloth in a covered container and refrigerate until needed.

oil to 1 cup of nonfat dry milk or skim milk.

★ **Buttermilk**—Add 1 tablespoon of lemon juice to one cup of lukewarm nonfat milk.

★ **Whipped cream**—Substitute whipped,

chilled evaporated milk.

★ **Cream cheese**—Blend 4 tablespoons of margarine with 1 cup of low-fat cottage cheese. For additional smoothness, add a few tablespoons of skim milk during the blending process.

Tactics for the Diet Conscious

In the final analysis, the key to creating tasty but sensible dishes is not about remembering tips and substitutions. Good-tasting food is the by-product of an awareness that makes healthy eating and vibrant living possible.

To get the most out of your cuisine, you can't go around feeling that you have deprived yourself. You must allow yourself to enjoy your food. And the key to enjoyment is living a balanced lifestyle. Listed below are a few simple guidelines to help you prepare healthy but sophisticated, delicious meals.

★ Eat sensibly but enjoy yourself when you're at the table.
★ Watch what you eat between meals so

that you can allow yourself indulgences at lunch or dinner time.

★ Eat less red meat. When you do have it, select the leaner cuts for your table.

★ Strive to take in more natural fiber in the form of fruits and vegetables.

★ Reduce the amount of sugar you take in. If you have a sweet tooth, build your desserts around fruit instead of baked goods and dairy-based desserts. If you do bake, use fruit juice as a sweetener.

★ When you're shopping, consciously seek out lower-calorie, lower-salt and higher-fiber foods.

★ Build your entrees around great ingredients, fragrant spices and low-fat cooking techniques.

Miscellaneous Calorie Savers

★ Before cooking meats, trim all visible fat from them.

★ Cook stews a day or two before you intend to serve them. Chill overnight and skim off the fat before you reheat.

★ For additional richness without additional fat, add powdered skim milk to mashed potatoes. Moisten the dish with broth instead of creamery butter.

★ To save more calories while baking, substitute nonfat dry milk for some of the sugar. A good rule of thumb in recipes for cookies, bars and cakes is to replace one-quarter of the sugar with the equivalent amount of nonfat dry milk. For example, if the recipe calls for 1 cup of sugar, use 3/4 cup of sugar and 1/4 cup of nonfat dry milk.

★ Whenever butter is called for in a recipe, use unsalted butter.

★ Where there is a choice, bake or broil your foods instead of frying them.

Cook Your Way to a Thinner Waist

Sauté the Fat Away

Everyone loves the richness of sautéed foods, but to those of us watching our weight or cholesterol, that delightful flounder fillet sautéed in butter is a temptation we can't afford. Does that mean we're condemned to eating broiled fish or vegetables? Absolutely not. All you have to do is change the medium in which you sauté. Instead of using butter or rich vegetable oils, try sautéing in broths, wine or stocks. They'll give a rich flavor to your dish without all the fat and calories, and they'll keep your favorite dish plenty moist during the cooking process.

Here's how: add enough stock or wine to cover the bottom of your pan and then bring it to a boil before adding your fillet or vegetables. Then cover your pan and reduce heat to medium. For best results, monitor the amount of liquid in your pan while sautéing. If your stock or broth begins to evaporate before the dish is done, add more liquid.

How to Thicken Sauces without Thickening Your Waist

The traditional way to create a nice thick sauce is to add ingredients such as flour until the sauce reaches the right consistency. In recent years, professional chefs have devised several alternatives that will save you calories.

Followers of the nouvelle cuisine school typically thicken their sauces by boiling them down or "reducing" them. Reduction not only thickens the sauce nicely, but also enhances its natural flavor.

Using a starch such as cornstarch or arrowroot is another alternative. Arrowroot

COOKING TIP #17 FROM THE CHEFS

Low-Fat Hollandaise Sauce

Here's a variation on everyone's favorite sauce, prepared with broth as a replacement for most of the butter. The end result is a great-tasting sauce with approximately one-third the calories.

4 tablespoons lemon juice
3/4 cup chicken stock (homemade or canned)
5 egg yolks
2 tablespoons butter, melted
1/4 teaspoon salt
pinch of cayenne pepper

Boil the lemon juice and chicken stock until reduced down to 3/4 cup; remove from the heat and allow to cool. In a separate saucepan, whisk the eggs yolks until foamy. Place the saucepan on low heat and slowly add the lemon and chicken stock mixture, whisking continuously until the sauce thickens. Remove from heat and stir in melted butter before seasoning to taste.

COOKING TIP #18 FROM THE CHEFS

"THIN" YOUR STOCK BEFORE SAUTÉING

If you're sautéing with stocks in order to cut fat, make sure you've removed all extraneous fat from your chicken or meat stock. Whether it's homemade or canned stock, refrigerate overnight. After the stock has gelled, skim the solidified fat from the surface. If you're extra vigilant, some experts advise pouring the stock through a funnel filled with ice cubes to capture the remaining fat.

is prized by many because it thickens soups and sauces and has less than a third of the calories found in flour. A word of caution: if you boil a sauce thickened with arrowroot or cornstarch for too long, your sauce may actually liquify rather than thicken.

This process is called hydrolyzing and can be avoided by keeping your sauce on moderate heat until it is finished.

Cooking with Food's Natural Moisture

Apart from taste, one of the most important features of a well-prepared dish is its

COOKING TIP #19 FROM THE CHEFS

Two No-fat Soup Thickeners

The traditional way to thicken a hearty winter soup is to add butter and flour or even eggs to the pot. A healthier technique is to puree a portion of the soup in your food processor or blender. When you stir it back into the pot, you'll have a thicker soup with enhanced flavor and texture. Another technique is to puree soft rice and add it to the soup to help hold it together and improve its texture.

texture and consistency. A great dish is never too dry, too chewy or too mushy, and the key to controlling these qualities is moisture. In traditional cooking, moisture was controlled through the use of calorie-laden sauces, fats and oils. Today's experts have an arsenal of other techniques at their disposal—the best of which follow.

The common grocery bag can be one of your biggest allies in the battle for moist, low-fat food. You can make the most delicious baked chicken imaginable by enclosing the bird in a grocery bag and then baking it in the oven at 350 degrees for an hour and a half. The paper bag keeps the chicken's natural moisture inside the bird rather than letting it evaporate. You end up with the equivalent of a self-basting chicken without all the extra fat. Don't worry: since paper ignites at 451 degrees, the bag won't burn.

There are plenty of commercial products that will accomplish the same thing, including parchment paper, aluminum foil and roasting bags. You can also use natural wraps, such as cabbage leaves and corn husks, to keep moisture in your food.

Surprisingly, salt can also be your ally in keeping the moisture in and the calorie content down. By encasing large pieces of fish, poultry or meat in a paste of coarse salt (look for Kosher salt in your market) and water, you will create a crust that accomplishes the same thing as a roasting bag. Take roughly two cups of salt per pound of meat, and add just enough water to create a paste. Place half the salt in the bottom of the roasting pan and then place the meat on top of it. Pack the remaining salt around the meat to create a shell, and then roast at the normal temperature for the meat. When the meat has reached the desired temperature, remove from the oven and let sit 5 to 10 minutes before cracking and discarding the salt crust. The salt will not dissolve into the food, and you will have a wonderfully moist and tender entree without the calories associated with sauces.

Poaching Not Just for Eggs Anymore

Most of us grew up eating the occasional poached egg for breakfast, especially when we wanted to avoid the calories associated with fried or scrambled eggs. Did you know that poaching can be applied to a variety of main courses, including fish, lamb, beef and chicken? All you have to do is simmer the fish or meat in bouillon made of water, herbs and chopped onions or scallions. Simmer until the meat is done. Remove the skin from chicken or fish, and serve with a low-calorie sauce.

Don't Sweat It, Steam It

Oriental cooking has given us one of the great tools for controlling calories—the bamboo steamer. Whether you choose a steamer made of traditional bamboo or one of the newer stainless steel baskets, there's simply no better way to bring out the natural flavors and rich colors of fresh produce. Like poaching, steaming is an

COOKING TIP #20 FROM THE CHEFS

FOR VARIETY, COLOR AND TASTE, PUREE YOUR VEGETABLES

A favorite calorie-saving technique of contemporary chefs is to serve pureed vegetables either alone or in combinations. Pureeing adds a richness in taste that makes adding butter or other sauces unnecessary.

outstanding method of preparing fish and poultry without added fat.

To use a steamer, place it on a saucepan filled with a couple of inches of water. Fill the basket with your meat or vegetables, cover and bring to a boil. Vegetables take 3 to 5 minutes, and fish and chicken take anywhere from 10 to 20 minutes depending on the thickness of the cut or fillet.

Bake or Broil
Instead of Frying or Sautéing

Another way chefs reduce fat and calories is to broil instead of fry. If you're browning chuck for a stew, place it in a broiling pan instead of the frying pan. This approach cuts fat in two ways: you're browning without adding fat, and much of the fat in the meat ends up as drippings in the broiling pan.

You can also use your oven and broiler pan to make lower-fat and better-looking bacon. Spread individual bacon pieces on the broiler, and broil in a 400-degree oven until crisp. Broiled bacon isn't as curly as fried bacon, and once again, most of the fat is in the broiling pan.

Prepare plump, low-fat meatballs by baking them on a cookie sheet rather than frying them. Twenty minutes in a 375-degree oven should do nicely.

French toast, French fries and even "fried chicken" can also be baked to save on fat and calories. For low-fat French toast, bake five minutes a side in a 400-degree oven.

Chicken pieces dredged in bread crumbs will bake nicely at 325 degrees for roughly an hour. And French fries will seem almost fried if you bake them on an oiled cookie sheet at 475 degrees for 35 minutes. Turn often for best results.

Indispensable Tools for Low-fat, Low-calorie Cooking

Start with a Nonstick Pan

If you're serious about healthier cooking, there are several additions you should make to the basic equipment in your kitchen.

First and foremost, acquire a nonstick pan or two. Use the same guidelines you would use when buying any other cookware. Whether it's coated with Silverstone, Teflon or some other nonstick surface is less important than the thickness of the pan itself. Buy the best you can afford, and make sure the pan is

COOKING TIP #21 FROM THE CHEFS

Home off the Range– Resurrecting the Backyard Grill

A basic technique of nouvelle cuisine and modern California cuisine alike is grilling. Grilling is a great way to add a rich, smoky flavor to your chops, steaks, chicken and vegetables without adding fats. Even if your range isn't equipped for grilling, don't despair. Your lowly backyard grill will do nicely.

heavy enough to distribute heat evenly. Thick aluminum pans distribute the heat evenly. With the cheaper, thinner models, expect the occasional burned entree.

Get a good food processor and a professional-quality blender for pureeing food and creating creamy sauces. Even though it seems as if they do the same job, the higher

speeds of blenders make them better at creating lighter, fluffier concoctions.

Try aerosol cooking sprays to reduce the
amount of fat necessary for baking,
sautéing and browning of meats. Today's
cooking sprays are available in a number of
flavors, including butter and olive oil.

Another alternative to traditional frying
or sautéing is stir-frying in a wok. The
wok's steep sides allow you to prepare
delicious dishes with virtually no oil. The
wok also doubles as a saucepan suitable
for poaching fish or poultry.

The Microwave

It's rare to find an American home without a microwave oven, but unfortunately
most families use them for little more
than making popcorn, reheating meals
and preparing prepackaged foods. If used
properly, the microwave oven can be a
great weapon in the battle against the
bulge. Instead of sautéing chopped
onions in butter or oil, microwave them
in a covered dish and save tons of calo-

ries. The microwave is also a great boon for preparing vegetables such as eggplant, which tend to absorb great amounts of oil if sautéed.

CHAPTER FIVE

Averting Culinary Disaster

Everything in Its Proper Place

The Keys to Averting Culinary Disaster

Beginning cooks, and sometimes even more experienced ones, often don't spend enough time in study and preparation for the big event. They leap into a complicated and perhaps expensive recipe like Teddy Roosevelt charging up San Juan Hill. They arrive without a clue of what's going to be required once they're in the heat of battle. Enthusiasm and excitement become despair, as mistakes and omissions turn what could have been a beautiful experience into a messy kitchen and a failure at the table.

Professional chefs, on the other hand, spend a vast amount of time reading recipes and cookbooks. They're not only looking for new ideas and refinements. They're also becoming as familiar as possible with ingredients and new procedures before they go to work in the kitchen. If you walked into a chef's office, you would see notebooks or journals filled with ideas for new dishes and reminders of techniques that improve on what they already know. Even a dish they've made a thousand times will be reviewed and considered before they begin. Remember that recipes are written in a compact, compressed style and the information may not be totally clear on the first go round. Good cooks do their best to leave nothing to chance so that they can be better prepared to deal with emergencies. You can do the same.

★ As you study the recipe, make a list of

ingredients and quantities.

* Visualize each step of the process. Consider every element including techniques, special equipment, order of ingredients and time required for each step.

* Think about other recipes you've done that may have similar techniques—and pitfalls. Remind yourself of how you resolved them.

* Make notes in the margins of the books explaining or reminding yourself of solutions or steps that may be slightly unclear in the cookbook.

* Pay attention to the details. Instructions that are very specific, such as those for adding liquids to a dish, are presented in precise detail because they're essential to the success of the recipe. Follow amounts of ingredients precisely the first time you try a recipe. Once you've tried it, and know why and how all the ingredients and techniques come together, you can begin to build your own themes and variations.

* Use every pot and pan you need to do the job. Don't fear the dirty dishes, but

COOKING TIP #22 FROM THE CHEFS

LEARN TO STAND A LITTLE HEAT

Professional chefs learn to withstand a certain amount of heat on their hands and fingers. Watch the cooking shows on television and you'll see that they sometimes even turn meat in a sauté pan with their fingers. Not that anyone is suggesting it's a good idea to pull French fries out of burning oil, but a little exposure is a good idea. It can help avert a disaster when, inevitably, you forget to grab a potholder or towel to remove a lid. You can train yourself little by little to not panic when you accidentally touch something hot.

do your best to stay ahead of the mess.
★ From the beginning, work to master the techniques in complicated recipes.

Once you've learned them, you'll discover how often they will apply to general cooking. As you build your arsenal of techniques you will find your skill level increasing and you'll begin to develop recipes of your own.

★ Allow yourself plenty of time to put the meal together. Do as much as possible in terms of preparation and assembly in advance.

★ Remember that it's fun.

But there's more to averting disaster in the kitchen than learning to anticipate and honing your cooking skills. It is also extremely important to cook only with fresh and healthy food and to maintain high standards of cleanliness and safety in the kitchen. Protect yourself and those with whom you share your food from illness by following some rules for basic safety in the kitchen.

> ## COOKING TIP #23 FROM THE CHEFS
>
> ### THE HEAT IS ON
>
> There's nothing more likely to cause a soufflé or roast to fail than an improperly preheated oven. Unfortunately, it's a part of the preparation that is often ignored or overlooked until it's too late. Proper cooking temperatures have been tested and retested. The right oven heat is key to browned meat and rising baked goods—so preheat.

Looking out for Number One— Safety in the Kitchen

A professional kitchen is a whirlwind of activity, with cooks and helpers bustling through hundreds of tasks. The atmosphere is chaotic, and there is always the danger of accidents and sometimes serious injury. While things are a little calmer in the home kitchen, it's wise to follow some professional safety tips in the kitchen.

★ Tie back loose hair and don't wear hanging jewelry. Roll up the sleeves of loose garments.

★ Respect your knives. Good knives are essential to successful cooking but they are dangerous tools. The sharper and better maintained the blade, the safer it is to use. Dull knives make the work harder and require more force to cut, heightening the risk of slips. Always work with the blade directed away from the hand, and do not become distracted from the task. Work at a comfortable pace. It takes time and practice to learn how to dice with the speed of lightning.

★ Don't leave sharp cutting tools in the bottom of a sink or on the edge of a counter.

★ Don't leave spoons in hot pans.

★ Turn pan handles toward the center of the stove so the handle can't be brushed and possibly knocked off the stove. Just be sure the handle isn't over another burner.

* Remove lids carefully to avoid being burned by steam.
* Don't use wet potholders—they can transmit heat and result in severe burns.
* Make sure food processors are turned off before changing blades. Remove blades carefully.
* Clean up as you go to eliminate clutter and to keep spaces open for placing hot pans.
* Drain hot grease into a container placed in the sink to reduce the risk of spills and burns.

Help is on the Way

Salvaging the Homemade Mayo

There's nothing better than a perfect homemade mayonnaise, and there's nothing worse than a homemade mayonnaise that has thinned. Sometimes it's because the oil was improperly added; sometimes the mayo has curdled from being in the refrigerator. In either event, the solution is simple. Put a tablespoon of Dijon mustard and a tablespoon of the mayo in a dish. Beat vigorously with a wire whip or electric mixer until they are creamed. Then slowly add the mixture to the rest of the mayo, drop by drop until it rethickens.

Don't Roux the Day—
Taking the Lumps out of Gravy

The best fix for lumpy gravy is to make it correctly from the beginning. Lumps occur because the flour or other thickening agent was not completely broken down and dissolved when you added it to the stock or pan drippings. The balls of flour begin to cook exactly as if you were making dumplings. If you don't have the time or the ingredients to start over, strain the lumps out of the gravy and return it to the heat. While it won't be perfect, the gravy will probably be acceptable.

The simple fact is that a smooth, creamy gravy is very easy to make. Cook to reduce the pan drippings to the amount of liquid called for in the recipe. Combine the thickening agent with 1/4 cup of either water or stock, and mix thoroughly until the thickener is completely dissolved. Slowly pour the mixture into the roasting pan, stirring constantly until thickened. At that point, add water or stock to get the desired amount of gravy. Cook until the gravy has reached the consistency you desire.

A variation on this that most chefs employ is to make what is called a roux. Place equal amounts of butter (or margarine) and flour in a sauté pan and cook over a low heat. Stir constantly until the elements are thoroughly mixed, brown in color, and have a nutty aroma. Then add a small amount of stock at a time, stirring briskly until the mixture has begun to thicken. Add the roux and liquid mixture to the gravy pan and stir over medium heat until the gravy is done.

Pressing Garlic Questions

A rule by which all chefs abide is to use the freshest ingredients available—and that includes garlic. As the garlic gets older, the tips tend to emit a woody aroma. Aging garlic also loses its potency and loses its distinctive smell. But there is another way to turn garlic into a culinary turn-off. Quality garlic presses are convenient and real time-savers in the kitchen. Unless they are made of high quality metal, however, they can react chemically with the garlic, causing a bad smell and transmitting some "off" flavors to food.

The truth is, garlic is quite easy to handle without a press. Chop a large quantity in a food processor or by hand. Place in a tightly lidded jar, cover with a little olive oil and store in the refrigerator. A simple way to chop individual cloves is to take the flat of a chef's knife and press the garlic clove into the cutting board until it splits. Remove the skin—it comes off easily—and chop the garlic.

When using garlic that is not going to be cooked, as in a fresh salsa, do not use a garlic press. It will almost certainly affect the flavor.

Why Are My Beans Still Hard? They've Been Cooking for Hours!

With the exploding popularity of Southwestern and Mexican cuisines, chefs at home and in the finest restaurants are discovering the versatility and beauty of one of

COOKING TIP #24
FROM THE CHEFS

IT'S NOT A CROCK!

Beans do beautifully in a Crockpot with a glass lid. Follow the instructions for slow cooking.

the world's oldest staples—beans. Beans are full of protein and are sponges for absorbing spices and flavor. While beans are well worth adding to the cook's repertoire, they are not easy to cook to perfection. A common complaint is that no matter how long they're cooked, they never seem quite done. And when beans are the centerpiece of an elaborate meal, that crunchy texture can diminish the meal's success. One alternative, and not a terrible one, is to use canned beans. But if you want to cook them from scratch, here are some tips from chefs who have spent a great deal of time perfecting the art—the ones who work down Mexico way.

★ It's common to hear that beans should

be soaked overnight in cold water to begin the softening process. For a faster alternative, try starting the process on the stove. Simmer the beans at a very low temperature from 2 to 4 hours, depending on the dryness of the beans. As the liquid evaporates, replenish it with water to cover.

★ Don't add salt until the beans are soft. It will toughen the skins.

★ Do not stir the beans with a metal spoon.

★ Beans are actually at their best a day after they've been cooked. After they've cooled, place them in the refrigerator and reheat them the next day. They'll be tender and succulent without being mushy.

Salt Fanatics Beware— There Is No Quick Fix for Oversalting!

Use salt sparingly. It's very difficult to save a stew or soup or sauce that has been oversalted. Many chefs advise adding salt early in the cooking process and not again until the final tasting. While it enhances the flavor of many foods, salt is also the destroyer. Never, but never, pour salt into a pot directly from the shaker or box. Pour a tiny amount in your hand, then sprinkle it in with your fingers.

If you've oversalted a soup or vegetables, add cut raw potatoes. Discard once they have cooked and absorbed the salt. A teaspoon each of cider vinegar and sugar added to salty soup or vegetables might also help remedy the salty situation.

What to Do When You Run out of an Ingredient

Emergency Substitutions

If you don't have that final important ingredient, it's just possible you won't have to send a loved one rushing to the all-night market. Following is a list of emergency substitutions that might save the day:

* 1 cup cake flour—Use 1 cup minus 2 tablespoons all-purpose flour.
* 1 tablespoon cornstarch—Use 2 tablespoons all-purpose flour (for thickening).
* 1 tablespoon arrowroot—Use 2 table-

spoons all-purpose flour or 1 tablespoon cornstarch.

★ 1 teaspoon baking powder—Use 1/2 teaspoon cream of tartar plus 1/4 teaspoon baking soda.

★ 1 cup granulated sugar—Use 1 cup firmly packed brown sugar or 2 cups sifted confectioner's sugar.

★ 1 cup honey—Use 1 cup sugar plus 1/4 cup milk or water.

★ 1 cup corn syrup—Use 1 cup sugar plus 1/4 cup milk or water.

★ 1 square (1 ounce) unsweetened chocolate—Use 3 tablespoons unsweetened cocoa powder plus 1 tablespoon vegetable shortening or cooking oil.

★ 1 cup heavy cream, whipped—Use 2 cups whipped dessert topping.

★ 1 cup light cream—Use 1 tablespoon melted butter plus enough milk to make 1 cup.

★ 1 cup dairy sour cream—Use 1 cup plain yogurt plus 3 tablespoons melted butter.

★ 1 cup reduced-fat buttermilk—Use 1 tablespoon lemon juice or vinegar plus enough 2% milk to make 1 cup. Let stand

5 minutes before using. You can also use 1 cup 2% milk plus 3/4 teaspoon cream of tartar, or 1 cup plain yogurt.

★ 1 cup whole buttermilk—Same as above, but use whole milk.

★ 1 cup whole milk—Use 1/2 cup evaporated milk plus 1/2 cup water, or 1 cup water plus 1/3 cup nonfat dry milk powder.

★ 1 cup canned tomatoes—Use 1 1/3 cups cut-up fresh tomatoes. Simmer 10 minutes.

★ 2 cups tomato sauce—Use 3/4 cup tomato paste plus 1 cup water.

★ 1 cup tomato juice—Use 1/2 cup tomato sauce plus 1/2 cup water.

★ 1 medium-size clove garlic—Use 1/8 teaspoon garlic powder.

★ 1 teaspoon chopped fresh ginger—Use 1/4 teaspoon ground ginger.

★ 1 tablespoon prepared mustard—Use 1 teaspoon ground mustard (in cooked mixtures).

★ 1 tablespoon fresh herbs—Use 1 teaspoon any dry leafy herbs.

★ 1 teaspoon grated fresh orange or lemon peel—Use slightly less, or equal amounts

of dehydrated lemon or orange peel.
* 1 teaspoon pure vanilla extract—Use 1 teaspoon vanilla powder.
* 1 teaspoon pure anise extract—Use 1 teaspoon anise seed.
* 5 teaspoons brandy—Use 1 teaspoon brandy extract.
* 1 tablespoon dark rum—Use 2 tablespoons rum extract.
* 5 tablespoons light rum—Use 1 tablespoon rum extract.
* 1 tablespoon sherry—Use 1 tablespoon pure sherry extract.

A Potpourri of Helpful Hints

Professional Solutions to Common Problems

Here's a little mixture of ideas that could save the day when things go wrong.

★ If you've over-sweetened a dish, add salt.
★ A teaspoon of cider vinegar will cut the sweet factor in main dishes or vegetables.
★ Pale gravy may be browned by adding a bit of instant coffee straight from the jar. It leaves no bitter taste.
★ The best method of removing fat from a sauce or soup is to refrigerate until the fat hardens. When you put it in the refrigerator, place a piece of waxed

paper on the surface of the food. When you peel off the paper, the hardened fat will come with it. Ice cubes will also eliminate the fat from soup and stew. Just drop a few into the pot and stir. The fat will cling to the cubes. Discard the cubes before they melt. Or try wrapping ice cubes in paper towel or cheesecloth. Skim across the top to remove fat.

★ A slice of soft bread placed in the package of hardened brown sugar will soften it again in a couple of hours. If you keep a cracker in the box, the sugar will remain soft.

★ A little salt or flour placed in a frying pan will prevent splattering.

★ Meat loaf will not stick to the pan if you place a slice of bacon on the bottom.

★ A few sticks of celery lining the bottom of the pan will keep braised meats from sticking.

★ Vinegar brought to a boil in a new frying pan will prevent foods from sticking.

★ When you're scalding milk, prevent sticking by rinsing your pan in cold water before putting milk in it.

★ A lump of butter or a few teaspoons of cooking oil added to water when boiling rice, noodles, macaroni, or spaghetti will prevent it from boiling over and will also keep the items from sticking together.

★ A few drops of lemon juice added to simmering rice will keep the grains separate.

★ A dampened paper towel or terry cloth brushed downward on a cob of corn will remove every strand of corn silk.

★ To determine if an egg is fresh, immerse it in a pan of cool, salted water. If it sinks, it is fresh. If it rises to the surface, throw it away. Fresh eggs' shells are rough and chalky. Old eggs are smooth and shiny.

★ To determine if an egg is hard-boiled, spin it. If it spins, it is hard-boiled. If it wobbles, it is raw or undercooked.

★ Eggshells can be easily removed from hard-boiled eggs if the cooking begins in cold salty water. Quickly immerse in cold water after they've boiled.

★ Bacon won't curl if you dip it into cold

water before frying.

★ To keep bacon slices from sticking together, roll the package into a tube shape and hold with rubber bands.

Roasting Right—Some Tips for a Perfect Prime Rib of Beef

A prime rib roasted to perfection is top-of-the-line to those who enjoy beef. And beef is making a comeback in the modern kitchen. But it's also one of the most expensive cuts in the butcher's case. There's nothing more frustrating than savoring the expectation of a perfectly done piece of meat only to find it under-cooked or, far worse, overcooked.

Most chefs begin a prime rib by searing it at a high temperature (500 degrees) for 15 minutes to seal in the juices. Then they lower the heat to 350 degrees and roast until done. A rule of thumb for timing with this method is 15 minutes per pound for rare, 20 minutes per pound for medium and 25 minutes per pound for well done.

An accurate meat thermometer is a

good tool for helping gauge the doneness, but most must be inserted from the beginning to give a trustworthy reading.

Give It a Rest, Brother

One of the most common errors cooks make when roasting meat of any kind is not allowing the meat to rest after it comes out of the oven and before it's carved. Resting allows the meat to reabsorb some of its juices, makes it easier to carve and enhances the texture and flavor. A roast beef should rest at least 15 minutes. Plan accordingly when you're putting the finishing touches on the meal. And remember that the roast will continue to cook and the internal temperature will rise at least five degrees while it rests.

Use Your Hand! Testing a Roast for Doneness

Caught without a meat thermometer? Not sure how long that expensive prime rib has been in the oven? There's a simple and almost foolproof way to test whether a roast is done and all it takes is your own two hands. The general rule is, the softer the meat feels when touched the rarer it is. Touch the roast in the center of a lean portion. Then compare it with the firmness of your hand:

★ **For Rare**—Let your hand dangle loosely, then shake it gently to relax the muscles. Touch your index finger into the soft flesh between the thumb and index finger of the relaxed hand. It will yield easily, the same way rare meat does.

★ **For Medium**—Stretch your hand and tense your fingers. When you touch the muscle it will feel firm and springy, like medium meat, and give some resistance to your index finger.

★ **For Well Done**—Ball your hand into a fist. Like a well-done roast, the muscle will feel hard and will not yield to the pressure of your finger.

COOKING TIP #25 FROM THE CHEFS

DON'T LET IT WEIGH ON YOUR MIND

It's amazing how often home cooks, even those who know that weight affects cooking time, will get home, rip the wrapping off the meat, and toss the wrapping away without reading the label. Knowing the weight is essential if you want to win the battle between your food and your oven.

Removing Acid from Tomato Sauces

If you make a tomato sauce and it has a strong acidic taste, try adding baking soda a pinch at a time until the flavor begins to even out. The baking soda may cause a foam to form on the surface, but it will disappear as you stir.

Good Health
in the Kitchen

Unwrap That Meat

If you're going to freeze meat or keep it in the refrigerator for more than two or three days, remove the store's plastic wrapping. Wash and rewrap in fresh plastic, freezer wrap, or aluminum foil. There is always a possibility of contamination from the store.

Thawing a Thanksgiving
Turkey Safely

The safest way to thaw any frozen food is in the refrigerator. It's essential with roasts, large birds like turkeys, and chicken of any kind. Of course, the best-tasting

and most easily cooked turkey is freshly
killed and ready for the oven. But if you
purchase a frozen turkey, you must allow
sufficient time to thaw it safely. For a
turkey in the 18-22 pound range, it is best
to allow five full days of time in your
refrigerator to thaw it out. Whether your
turkey is fresh or frozen, be sure to
remove the giblet pack and neck from
inside the cavity and neck openings.
Before cooking, rinse the turkey inside
and out with cool water and pat dry.
Check to be sure the turkey fits the roaster you intend to cook it in.

Don't Give Them Critters Any Place to Hide

Unless your bird is going right into the
oven, don't stuff it with room temperature
stuffing. It's a breeding ground for bacteria and contamination. Avoid the risk
altogether by cooking the stuffing in a
separate pan.

Avoiding Poultry Problems—
Salmonella and You

Chicken is one of the world's most popular meats. It's inexpensive, versatile, and a good source of healthy protein. The United States consumes almost six billion chickens a year and the industry is hard-pressed to keep up with the demand. This vast production has resulted in a high rate of salmonella contamination in poultry shipped to market. The National Academy of Sciences estimates that 48 percent of food poisoning is caused by contaminated chicken. On a personal level that means 1 in 50 people is affected annually.

What is salmonella, anyway? Salmonella is a fragile type of bacteria transmitted by pets, rodents, insects, human beings and other animals. It is strongly drawn to poultry and contaminates it quickly. The bacteria can live in frozen food but are inactive up to 45 degrees and die quickly at temperatures above 140 degrees. Higher temperatures kill them even faster. Common sense and care can take salmonella out of your food and out of your life.

You can enjoy and trust your favorite chicken dishes if you follow a few simple guidelines:

* Buy the freshest product you can, if not from a butcher, then make sure the dates on the package are current.
* Trust your eye and nose to tell you if it's fresh. Chicken should have a fresh smell and a bright look. Pass it by if you have any doubts.
* Thaw frozen chicken completely in the refrigerator or microwave oven—not in water in the sink.
* Clean all work surfaces (including the sink) thoroughly with hot soapy water before using them for other tasks such as chopping or rinsing vegetables.
* If you have used a kitchen towel to wipe hands or knives, put it in the laundry.
* Wash hands, knives and other utensils thoroughly after prepping chicken.
* Follow guidelines for proper cooking temperatures carefully.
* Refrigerate leftovers immediately after use.

Wash That Pesky
Can Opener, Too

One kitchen implement often overlooked during cleanup is the can opener. The blades and gears can quickly become contaminated from particles of food left behind and become a source of food poisoning.

Why You Should Refrigerate
Products That Don't Require It

Many salad dressings, mustards, mayos and the like state clearly on the label that no refrigeration is necessary. Technically that's true, but here's the kicker. While the products themselves are fine on the shelf, you add particles of food to them every time you spread some and then plunge the knife back in the jar. That food may not stand up so well. Best to keep everything cool.

General Tips

It's All Different When You Reach the Heights— High-Altitude Cooking

If you live higher than 1,000 feet above sea level, the rules for cooking times and temperatures go right out the window. It's deceptive, but as you go higher, water begins to boil at a lower temperature. The higher you go the worse it gets. It's wise to invest in a cookbook that specializes in tips and conversions for altitude, so you can adjust your favorite recipes and raise them to new heights of perfection.

An Emergency Roasting Rack

Birds roast better if they are cooked on a

rack. If you don't have one big enough for a large bird, here's a quick and easy solution. Tear a long strip of aluminum foil from the roll. Roll it into a tube like a newspaper, then form it into a ring about six inches in diameter. Place the ring in the bottom of your roaster and place the bird on the ring. Promise yourself that next year you'll spring for a rack.

Don't Wine to Me about It

While they're fine for deglazing to make a wine sauce, black iron or aluminum pots will affect the taste of foods simmered in wine. Use stainless steel, ceramic or porcelain-covered cast iron.

The Problems with COOKING WINE as opposed to COOKING with WINE

Cooking with wine adds complexity and subtle variety to the taste of foods. Those who object to alcohol but are not in danger from alcohol need not worry—the alcohol evaporates almost immediately during cooking. Only the flavor remains. If you can't tolerate alcohol for health reasons, however, it's best not to cook with wine. Don't substitute so-called "cooking wines" and expect them to be a decent alternative either. Avoid "cooking wine" at all costs. It is packed with salt in order to get around the laws surrounding the taxation and shipment of alcohol. One taste will tell you it isn't something you want in your food.

Something's Fishy— Getting Rid of That Smell from Your Cooking Oil

If you deep-fry fish, the oil will inevitably begin to create an unpleasant smell. The offensive odor can be eliminated by frying several pieces of ginger root for a few minutes. It will cleanse and invigorate the cooking oil and your kitchen will smell fresher.

Organize Those Ingredients

A sure way to avoid last-minute disasters in the kitchen is to set aside an area in the kitchen to organize cooking implements and ingredients. Before you begin cooking, have all preparations finished and in place so that you can concentrate on making a great meal instead of wondering where the oregano is at a crucial moment.

Organize your kitchen and all your cooking tools to suit your tastes. Keep it organized to eliminate clutter and last minute searches.

Proper Knife Technique

To protect yourself while cutting with a sharp knife, hold the knife securely and keep your fingers out of the way of the blade. The chef's technique is to grasp the knife at the end of the blade with the forefinger and thumb and balance the rest of the hand on top of the handle. The other hand holds the food firmly with fingers bent underneath the hand and away from the blade.

Chopping motions should be efficient and controlled. Learn to keep the tip of the blade on the cutting surface and use it as a pivot while you chop.

The Road to Confidence in the Kitchen

Think about What You're Doing and Why You're Doing It

Even the greatest chefs find ways to improve their techniques almost every day in the kitchen. Work to improve all your skills and be open to new ideas. Don't hold onto anything out of stubbornness.

Don't make assumptions or take things for granted. Just because French fries and hamburgers with ketchup are a classic combination, don't reject the idea of a good hot salsa with fresh tomatoes and blue corn tortilla chips as an alternative.

Try out new things constantly. Ideas about making and serving food always evolve. The best chefs always wonder whether this would go with that, despite what conventional wisdom might say. You'll never know whether or not you've invented a new taste treat unless you spend some time in the kitchen trying it out.

Make a recipe many times. Become patient and precise and continue to perfect your favorite foods. Consistent attempts are necessary for you to learn how ingredients go together and how things can go wrong. Small changes can affect the results greatly, often for the worse, but sometimes you'll discover a variation that is far superior to the original dish.

Learn how long it takes to do things. As your cooking skills increase, you will attempt more complicated recipes that demand a series of steps in rapid order. You should know how long it takes to slice a pound of tomatoes or chop seven cloves of garlic, so that you can be in control of a most essential element—timing.

Explore, Explore, Explore. Don't allow yourself to become bored with your own cooking. Try new restaurants and cuisines. Try foods that are not your usual choice, and taste a wide variety of wines and beverages. Take advantage of the explosion of cooking shows on cable television to get new food ideas. Look carefully over the entire menu of your favorite restaurant, rather than automatically going to what you always order.

Respect and enjoy your work in the kitchen. If you love to cook, you know the pleasure of preparation and the joy of watching others enjoy your food. Cooking well is an act of love. Far more than a necessity or a hobby, it's one of the greatest satisfactions in life.

Index of Cooking Tips From the Chefs

Index of Recipes

Glossary

ADJUST–The final taste before serving to correct seasonings.

AL DENTE–Italian idiom meaning "to the tooth." Refers to pasta cooked to the point of being tender but still firm.

AU JUS–The serving of meats in their roasting juices.

BASTE–To ladle or brush pan dripping on meat while it is roasting to keep it from drying out and to add flavor.

BATTERIE DE CUISINE–All of the tools and implements necessary for cooking.

BIND–To stir egg, sauce, or another thickening ingredient into a mixture to hold it together.

BLANCH–To immerse briefly in boiling water to loosen skins or to set flavor and color. Usually refers to vegetables.

BRAISE–To brown in fat before cooking covered, either on the stovetop or in the oven.

BRUISE–To partially crush (as garlic) in order to release flavor.

CHIFFONADE–A garnish of finely cut vegetable strips. Usually, but not always, for soups.

CHOP–To cut into small pieces. The result is a coarser product than one that is minced.

COAT A SPOON–A test for doneness for custards and other egg-thickened mixtures. A properly cooked mixture will leave a thin film on a metal spoon.

CODDLE–To poach in water just below the boiling point.

COOL–To bring hot food to room temperature. As opposed to CHILL which means to place in the refrigerator to quickly bring down the temperature.

CRUMBLE–To break up with the fingers.

CRUSH–To reduce to crumbs.

CUBE–To cut into cube shapes of a consistent size.

CURE–To preserve meat, fish or cheese by salting, drying or smoking.

CUT IN–To mix shortening or other solid fat into dry ingredients until the texture is coarse and mealy.

DEGLAZE–To scrape the browned bits off the bottom of a skillet or roasting pan in a small amount of liquid using gentle to medium heat. The result is mixed into a gravy or served alone as an accompaniment to the dish.

DEGREASE–To remove grease from liquid by skimming or blotting.

DEVIL–To mix with hot seasonings.

DICE–To cut into small cubes. (1/8" to 1/4")

DILUTE–To weaken or thin by adding liquid.

DOT–To distribute small bits of butter over the surface of a food.

DREDGE–To coat lightly with flour, confectioners' sugar or other fine powder.

DRIZZLE–To pour melted butter, syrup or sauce over a dish in a thin, steady stream.

ENTREE–Main course of a meal.

ESSENSE/EXTRACT–Concentrated flavoring.

FILLET–A boneless piece of meat or fish.

FILTER–To strain a liquid through several thicknesses of cheesecloth in order to remove bits and pieces in the liquid.

FINISH–To add the final garnish to a dish before serving.

FLAKE–To break into small pieces with a fork.

FROMAGE–French word for cheese.

FUMET–A concentrated stock used for sauces.

GARNISH–To decorate a dish before serving.

GRATE–To cut food into tiny particles with a grater. Often cheese.

HUSK–To remove the coarse outer covering of a vegetable.

ICE–To spread frosting on a cake or pastry. Or to chill until hard.

INFUSE–To steep herbs, spices, coffee or tea in hot liquid in order for the liquid to gather their flavor.

JELL (OR GEL)–To bind a liquid with gelatin, as in an aspic.

KNEAD–To work with the hands in a rhythmic pattern until the dough is smooth and thoroughly blended.

LARD–To insert bits of lard or other fat into lean meat to keep it moist and to add flavor.

LET DOWN–To dilute by adding liquid.

LINE–To cover the bottom and sides of a pan or mold with wax paper or crumbs before adding the food.

MACERATE–To soak fruits in alcoholic spirits.

MARINATE–To steep foods in flavored liquids before cooking to add flavor and tenderize.

MASH–To reduce foods such as potatoes to pulp.

MASK–To coat foods with a sauce or aspic.

MEDALLION–Small, coin-shaped piece of meat, usually beef.

MINCE–To cut foods into fine pieces.

MOLD–To prepare foods in a shaped mold for presentation.

MULL–To heat fruit juices, wines, ales or hard liquor with spices and sugar.

NAP–To coat with sauce.

NOISETTE–A small piece of meat, usually lamb.

OEUF–French word for egg.

PANBROIL–To cook in a skillet over direct heat with as little fat as possible. Juices are drained as they accumulate.

PANFRY (SAUTÉ)–To cook in a skillet with some fat without pouring off the drippings.

PARCH–To dry by roasting, usually starchy vegetables.

PARE–To remove the peelings from fruits and vegetables. Also **PEEL**.

PASTE–A smooth blend of fat and flour or other starchy thickener.

PINCH–The amount of seasoning that can be held between the thumb and forefinger. Less than 1/8 teaspoon.

PLANK–To broil meats, fish or vegetables on a wooden plank.

PLUMP–To soak dried fruits or vegetables in liquid until they soften and regain some of their original form.

POACH–To cook submerged in a simmering liquid.

POULET–French word for chicken.

PREHEAT–To bring an oven to the required temperature before adding food.

PRICK–To pierce the surface of a dish to release steam or fat.

PUREE–To grind to a paste using a food mill, blender or food processor.

QUENELLES–Poached forcemeat dumplings used as a garnish for fish or meat.

RAGOUT–A hearty stew.

RAMEKIN–A small, single-serving baking dish.

REDUCE–To boil a liquid down rapidly to concentrate flavors.

REFRESH–To plunge hot food, usually vegetables, into cold water to stop the cooking process and retain color and flavor.

ROAST–To cook uncovered in an oven using dry heat.

ROE–Fish eggs.

ROUX–A paste of flour and water used as a thickener for sauces.

SAUTÉ–See **PANFRY**.

SCALD–To heat a liquid just to the point of boiling, usually milk. Also to plunge skinned fruits or vegetables into boiling water to ease the removal of skin.

SCORE–To make shallow knife cuts over the surface of a food in a crisscross pattern.

SEAR–To brown meat very quickly over high heat either in the oven or in a skillet.

SET, SET UP–To congeal as when a thickening agent has been added.

SHRED–To cut in small, thin strips by forcing through a grater.

SIMMER–To heat a liquid until bubbles just begin to form.

SLIVER–To cut in fine thin pieces less than 1/2 inch long and a fraction of that wide.

STEAM–To cook covered over a small amount of boiling water so that the steam cooks the food.

STOCK–The broth strained from stewed or boiled meats, seafood, poultry or vegetables.

STRAIN–To separate liquids by passing them through a sieve.

STUD–To insert cloves or slivers of garlic, clove or other seasoning over the surface of a food.

TRUSS–To tie poultry or meats into a compact shape before roasting.

VENT–To create an opening in a pastry shell allowing the release of steam.

WHIP–To beat until stiff, usually with a whisk.

WORK–To mix slowly with the fingers.

ZEST–The colored part of a citrus rind used as a flavoring.

TAYLOR SMITH

Who would you trust with your life?
Think again.

A tranquil New England town is rocked to its core when a young coed is linked to a devastating crime—then goes missing.

One woman, who believes in the girl's innocence, is determined to find her before she's silenced—forever. Her only ally is a man who no longer believes in anyone's innocence. But *is* he an ally?

At a time when all loyalties are suspect, and old friends may be foes, she has to decide—quickly—who can be trusted. The wrong choice could be fatal.

THE
BEST OF
ENEMIES

Available at your favorite retail outlet
in June 1997.

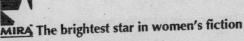

MIRA The brightest star in women's fiction

MTSTBE-R

HE SAID

♥

SHE SAID

Explore the mystery of male/female communication in this extraordinary new book from two of your favorite Harlequin authors.

Jasmine Cresswell and Margaret St. George bring you the exciting story of two romantic adversaries—each from their own point of view!

DEV'S STORY. CATHY'S STORY.
As he sees it. As she sees it.
Both sides of the story!

The heat is definitely on, and these two can't stay out of the kitchen!

Don't miss **HE SAID, SHE SAID.**
Available in July wherever Harlequin books are sold.

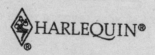

HARLEQUIN®

Look us up on-line at: http://www.romance.net

HESAID

And the Winner Is...
You!

...when you pick up these great titles
from our new promotion at your
favorite retail outlet this June!

Diana Palmer
The Case of the Mesmerizing Boss

Betty Neels
The Convenient Wife

Annette Broadrick
Irresistible

Emma Darcy
A Wedding to Remember

Rachel Lee
Lost Warriors

Marie Ferrarella
Father Goose

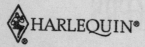 

Look us up on-line at: http://www.romance.net   ATWI397-R

From the bestselling author of
Iron Lace and *Rising Tides*

EMILIE RICHARDS

JANET DAILEY AWARD WINNER

When had the love and promises they'd shared turned into conversations they couldn't face, feelings they couldn't accept?

Samantha doesn't know how to fight the demons that have come between her and her husband, Joe. But she does know how to fight for something she wants: a child.

But the trouble is Joe. Can he accept that he'll never be the man he's expected to be—and can he seize this one chance at happiness that may never come again?

THE TROUBLE WITH JOE

"A great read and a winner in every sense of the word!"
—Janet Dailey

Available in June 1997
at your favorite retail outlet.

MIRA The brightest star in women's fiction

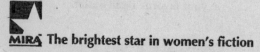